MW01244175

Red Beans & Ripcords

By

Mike Marcon

Cover photo: The author sitting atop a Cessna 170
N5587C circa 1968.

Photo taken by Leon

Copyright @ 2011 Mike Marcon

ISBN-13:978-1463550264

Marcon Publishing
Heathsville, Virginia
info@mikemarcon.info

For my wife, Marianne, who puts up with it.

About the Author

In the summer of 1962, the young Mike Marcon was lying on his bunk at Ft. Bragg, half asleep, staring at the ceiling. Suddenly, the thunderous sound of someone running up the stairs of the two-story World War II era barracks he called "home," grew loud in his ear. It was a buddy from the second squad downstairs coming to share news.

The friend was going to learn how to make a sport parachute jump the next week-end. He wanted to know if Mike wanted to join him. Mike said he was in.

That would be the beginning of a long and exciting journey that would last for many years to come. The pursuit of the next jump, the next adventure would become his life blood. He would come to know many colorful characters and personalities who jumped alongside him. Tales of some of them are recounted here.

He put off the writing of these stories for years as he became older. He retired in 2007 and knew this book would no longer wait. This first book is about the early days of the world of sport parachuting and his involvement in it. He is now working on the follow-up book.

Mike has been published by Random House, Prentice-Hall, Hilltop Publishers and a number of smaller presses in addition to many magazines and newspapers. He now operates his own publishing company.

Introduction

Red Beans & Ripcords

They're called "Skydivers" today. But we used to be called "Sport Parachutists." I prefer the simple term, "jumper." The places we jumped were and are called "Drop Zones." This is where you landed when you jumped. A drop zone's personality was usually due to whoever owned or operated it and the way they conducted business. The real "flavor" of a drop zone came from the various personalities that showed up on the weekends when most of the activity took place.

At the start of the Twentieth Century, a very few kindred souls like "Tiny" Broadwick or Georgia Broadwick, her actual name, were the real pioneers. She was nicknamed 'Tiny' as she weighed only eighty-five pounds and was 4 feet tall. Born Georgia Ann Thompson, at the age of 15 she saw Charles Broadwick's World Famous Aeronauts parachute from a hot air balloon and decided to join the travelling troupe. She later became Broadwick's adopted daughter.

Among her many achievements, she was the first woman to parachute from an airplane on June 21, 1913, jumping from a plane built and piloted by Glenn L. Martin, 1,000 feet over Griffith Park in Los Angeles. She was also the first woman to parachute into water.

Other "pioneers," particularly after World War II, began jumping in small groups at military bases and at civilian airfields scattered around the country until the early 1960's when the sport really began to take off. I was first initiated into the sport in 1962 at Fort Bragg, North Carolina, the home of the 82nd Airborne Division. I made a few sport jumps there, then I was transferred to Germany and made no jumps for several years until I got back to the states.

In 1966, I returned from my first tour in the military and decided to get out and follow my passion, sport parachuting. I worked at minor part-time jobs, and then threw myself head long into what, today, is called "skydiving." Let me give you a look at the state of sport parachuting aka skydiving in the early to the mid 1960's. For many jumpers then, especially civilians, it went something like this.

In 1957, the first commercial skydiving schools began to appear, but these commercial operations were few and far between. The National Parachute Riggers-Jumpers, Incorporated, was an organized regulating body that started in the 1930's and later became the Parachute Club of America. PCA renamed itself the United States Parachute Association in 1967. However, up until about 1965, whether or not you were a member of any organization was of little consequence.

In time, drop zones, commercial centers and various clubs begin to require a USPA membership. Jumpers had started to realize that the Federal Aviation Administration was increasingly looking harder and harder at regulating sport parachuting, and skydivers knew that they needed a national lobbying body to keep from being regulated out of the sky. The USPA also knew that skydiving was quickly gaining popularity and more stringent training guidelines and safety regulations were necessary.

But prior to 1965, it was pretty much a whatever-you-could-get-away-with affair. Parachutes, for the most part, were all military surplus and if it inflated and seemed airworthy, you jumped it. As a civilian, I never gave much thought to the condition of parachutes until about 1966.

Clubs sprang up here and there, mostly at rural airstrips. Those clubs consisted of small batches of people who gathered on week-ends to jump together with little attention to safety, and they were usually not a formal organization with a charter and rules.

You pretty much took someone at their word when they told you how many jumps they had or how experienced they were until such time as they did something to prove otherwise. For example, few people concerned themselves with log books in the early days. Later, log books would become extremely important to validate certain kinds of jumps and what you did during those jumps. Those log books provided places to enter the jump number, altitudes, maneuvers performed, whether it was a day or night jump, or whether it was a jump into water or a terra firma landing and other pertinent information.

In time, all of that information, which had to be verified by the signature of another jumper, would be important for certain awards or licenses. Not having the proper level of licensure could prevent you from performing different types of jumps such as making a demonstration jump over a crowd or into differing kinds of locations.

My reentry into jumping after leaving the military was a prime example of how loose things could be. Once home, I got a job and spent my spare time clubbing around at night visiting various honkytonks around the south Mississippi coast. At one of those clubs, I met a guy named Rusty and we became good friends. The very first time we struck up a conversation, he asked me out-of-the-blue had I ever skydived. I answered in the absolute. He then asked me if I wanted to join him the coming weekend at an "airport" up in Lucedale, Mississippi. I gleefully answered that I'd be there bright and early.

That Saturday morning, I showed up at the "airport" which was nothing more than an expansive field with what appeared to be a ramshackle hangar near the road. Just outside of the hangar sat a dirty, dented small airplane with the right door taken off. Some guy was sitting in the open door of the airplane strumming a guitar and singing songs to a gaggle of young girls gathered around him. Off to the other side of the hangar were parked four or five cars and a few people milling about. I parked my car, got out and looked for Rusty.

He hadn't shown up yet, but one of the people wandering around the cars spotted me and approached.

We shook hands. His name was Noel. He told me, without being prompted, that he was the senior jumper there. I took that as gospel.

In those days, when someone told me that they were a jumper, I pretty much didn't challenge it unless they were wearing their helmet backwards. I just went along with the program. Shortly, Rusty pulled up and jumped out of his car and began introducing me to some of the others gathered there. "You ready to make a leap?" Rusty asked of me. I answered in the affirmative. "He then said, "Let's find you some gear."

No one asked me how many jumps I had made. First of all, the jumps I had made were two years prior and I had only made three sport jumps. Nowadays, you're considered a student well beyond your fiftieth jump. Even back then, at the commercial centers, you needed to make at least five jumps with your parachute automatically opened for you. Once you were cleared to pull your own ripcord, you progressed along a path of making free-fall jumps of varying lengths, from five second free-falls up to 30 second free-falls, all very carefully observed and critiqued.

I had three jumps and Rusty was digging up some gear for me – no questions asked. Hell, I didn't even know what Rusty's qualifications were or how many jumps he had made.

Shortly, Rusty came along with a main parachute slung over his shoulder, carrying a smaller reserve parachute in his hand. "Here ya go!" Rusty said enthusiastically. I took the gear and began putting it on. At least, I remembered how to do that. He had also dug up a helmet that was at least two sizes too big for me. In the meantime, I was frantically trying to remember everything I had learned two years before. Then Rusty said, "Let's do a thirty second delay."

That meant that on my fourth sport parachute jump ever, we would exit at 7,200 feet and free fall for 30 seconds and then I would, hopefully, open my parachute. I said, "Okay." Now, if you've never jumped, here's a little reader-participation exercise to give you a very small idea of what free falling for 30 seconds is like. First, imagine you are falling. You're in mid-air and the earth is far below you. Now, look at your watch for thirty seconds. You'll get some sense of long that is. The funny part? It never seems that long.

Now, here's what I was about to do that day. I was going to strap on a parachute, actually two of them, that I knew nothing about. I didn't know who packed them or how long ago they had been packed. I was going to get into a raggedy little airplane with a pilot who I knew nothing about along with two other jumpers whose qualifications or experience I knew nothing about.

Then, I was going to graduate from making three jumps at 2,500 feet with a parachute that had been automatically opened for me two years prior, to flinging myself out of that airplane that day at 7,200 feet and flailing around in free-fall for 30 seconds, hoping that when my altimeter read 2,500 feet, I could find a ripcord to pull and save my life. Did I consider any of that? Nope. Not one shred of it. Here's what I was thinking that day: *I'm just going watch them and do whatever they do.* That's it.

When the time came to exit, it was as if some magical force entered my mind and body. I mimicked every move the other guys did. I was last out, so that gave me an edge in the impersonation department. Upon exiting, they went into a spread eagle. I arched hard and did exactly as they did. I was completely stable – comfortable.

It was as if I had done it a thousand times. There was an adrenalin rush as I fell, but it felt good. I really don't remember looking at my altimeter. Doing so would have meant taking my eyes off of the other two guys. I remember the rapid rustling of the fabric of my clothes and the sound in my ears. I remember the wind getting underneath my helmet and trying to pull it off of my head. I watched as they both moved their arms inward towards their bodies to grasp their ripcords and I did the same. As they quickly pulled their arms back out, ripcords in hand, and their parachutes began to open, I copied their movements. It was if I had been born to skydive.

I found my ripcord, pulled it and my parachute opened. I then looked up into a completely foreign scene as I had absolutely no idea what I was supposed to be seeing. Whereas my parachutes at Fort Bragg years before had two slots to channel the air for steering, this one had two large L's cut from the fabric. But, it was full and round and that's all I cared about. I reached up and grabbed the steering toggles. Pulling one left would turn me left – pulling one right would turn me right. In no time, I hit the ground hard but was able to stand up immediately. The others came running over to me and we all began rapid-fire chatter about our experience.

The entire act was as natural as breathing. I was elated and hooked even more than before, already planning to go again. And, that's exactly what I did weekend after weekend for the next several months. I started picking up on the smaller nuances of skydiving and got proficient at packing parachutes. My mind was at all times filled with thoughts of the next jump.

The sport would refine itself over and over in the coming years with more regulations, better equipment, and jumpers who knew that if we were to survive as a sport, we would have to become much more sophisticated and less lawless. That would take time. Today, equipment development has progressed at light speed, with parachutes becoming smaller, lighter and, in some cases, faster and more dangerous.

Whereas the older parachutes merely let you down with little directional control, today's parachutes are square airfoils which mimic an airplane's wing. They reach much higher forward speeds and are extremely maneuverable. They have to be flown much the same way as an airplane. Landing accuracy has reached a point where it takes electronic measuring equipment to measure the miniscule distances that define who lands with more accuracy.

Aircraft sizes and capacities have increased to the point where as many as 100 jumpers can exit an airplane nearly simultaneously on one pass, instead of only three or four jumpers at a time as in the past. Even jumpsuits have improved. Additionally, most jumpers wear highly refined automatic openers that will save a life in the event of a collision or a black out that might incapacitate a jumper. The rules and regulations have increased as well. The United States Parachute Association is located just two hours from where I sit now, and has become a gold standard in how a sport should be run. But that's now.

The days of seedy airplanes and ex-military bulky equipment and poorly run clubs and drop zones are over. What is not over, if I could again put my feet into the boots of a first-time skydiver, is the thrill, the excitement and the camaraderie. I don't think that will ever fade away. I was in the thick of something new, crazy and wild in those days and I was completely immersed by it.

In 1966, the Viet Nam War, the assassinations of Martin Luther King and Bobby Kennedy and a host of other world events would rock our society and I would barely be aware of it. Neither were my fellow jumpers. We were in our own world.

We ate, slept and breathed rip-stop nylon, airplanes, high altitudes, and landing accurately. And, we had the reputation of being fierce revelers.

We were totally wrapped up in the sport and thought about little else. While the world was supposedly falling apart around us, we went on obliviously doing what we loved. I would continue that journey for more than 25 years. No matter where I jumped, there were encounters with memorable characters at every drop zone. They shaped my life and I have never recovered.

Mike Marcon

Chapter One

The Golden Eagles

After jumping at Lucedale for a while, I received an invitation to jump with another "club." They were the "The Golden Eagles" operating at a dinky airstrip near Ocean Springs, in south Mississippi.

Their drop zone was a swampy field way back in the woods half covered by scraggly young pine trees each about ten feet tall. It was a few miles away from the airstrip. The tricky part was not getting one of those trees up your behind on landing. Once you landed, you pulled what was left of your parachute out of the trees then spent the next three hours patching the holes the trees had torn in it before you could use it again. But we had fun.

One of that club's jumpers was a U.S. Air Force Tech Sergeant named Swartz who was stationed at nearby Keesler Air Force base. He had a young family -- a wife and two little kids. A stocky, short, friendly guy, Swartz had decided that he wanted the family dog to jump with him. He spent hours sitting at a heavy duty sewing machine making a special harness for the dog, a scruffy half breed mongrel that looked kind of like Benji.

Well, Swartz made several successful jumps with the dog. The procedure was that Swartz would leave the airplane with the dog cradled in his arms. Then, at the right altitude, Swartz would push the dog away and its parachute would open. Swartz would then pull his own ripcord and the two would float down together.

The method Swartz used to open the dog's parachute was the standard military way of automatically opening a parachute when someone jumps from a plane. The dog's parachute had what is known as a "static line" attached to it. A static line is usually about twelve feet long. One end of the static line is attached to the aircraft and the other end is attached to the parachute pack with breakable cord.

When the jumper, or dog, in this case, jumped and got to the end of the static line, the cord would break and the pack would be opened and out the parachute would come. The method is still is in use by the military today.

Now, it has to be stated that our equipment was questionable. All of it was military surplus, some of it twenty years old or older. Most of us had no money to buy new equipment and so relied on surplus gear. Swartz's gear was no different.

The static line he was using was made of cotton instead of nylon like those of today. It was probably made in the 40's.

So, Saturday morning comes and we all meet at the airport to load up. Swartz had the mutt all ready to go. Swartz's wife and kids are with him as well. I would be the first one to exit the airplane. We load up. I'll do a hop-and-pop -- that is, jump and immediately open my parachute. Then the airplane would circle back around, climb to a little higher altitude, and then Swartz and the dog would exit with the third jumper behind them. The dog didn't seem the least bit nervous.

While we were climbing out, I happened to notice that the dog had actually fallen asleep. Once at altitude, on jump run, I checked my spot, the place over the drop zone where I would exit. I gave the pilot a few minor heading changes to make, checked my gear quickly and sat in the door ready to go. When I was satisfied I was over the spot, I left the aircraft. I immediately pulled my ripcord and watched over my shoulder as my white, olive drab and orange canopy opened bringing me to a stop with a gentle tug.

I secured my ripcord, made sure I was drifting on the right line of descent and then hung under my parachute watching as the airplane circled back around to a position about five hundred feet above me. I saw Swartz sitting in the door cradling the dog. Once just past me, they exited.

Swartz arched into a spread and went into a short free-fall and then pushed the dog away as he opened his own parachute. The dog fell away, reached the end of the static line and the static line broke with an audible "pop!" The dog went into a spinning free fall and whistled all the way into the ground at terminal velocity. He never had a chance.

The three of us landed, minus the dog. I was busy aiming for the drop zone, and I never saw where he went -- neither did anyone else.

We all felt terrible. The wife and kids were back at the airport some miles away. A truck was waiting to pick us up and we all clambered in and rode in silence back to airport sans the dog. When we arrived, the kids came running up to the truck. "Where's Scruffy? Where's Scruffy!?" they anxiously inquired. We looked at Swartz. This was his problem to deal with.

There was a long pregnant pause. He then shrugged his shoulders and said in all mock earnestness, "He ran away. We couldn't find him."

The kids started to cry. "But, Daddy, we love him!" Swartz was starting to crumble; I could see his mouth quivering. I piped up. "I'm going to go back and look for him later. I'm sure he's fine. I'll find him. I promise."

Step One: Open big mouth. Step Two: Stick foot firmly in. But, I needed time. "First, let's get something to eat. I'm hungry." That shut them up for a while. Well, something to eat was accompanied by several six packs and jumping ended for the day.

The kids ate their hot dogs quietly but every now and then one of them would tear-up and ask again about the whereabouts of the now dead dog. I quelled them by saying, "He's probably at some farmer's house having a great time." That was accompanied by other nefarious lies to assuage them. Swartz was keeping quiet and shooting me panicky *What are we gonna do?* glances.

After a while, Swartz outstretched his arms and yawned a fake yawn, and said, "Kids, let's go home. Mike will find the dog and bring him home."

And, with that, he had officially handed me the problem, which I wouldn't have had if I had kept my mouth shut.

I was single then, loved camp fires and on the week-ends usually overnighted in a tent at the airport. The cooler was full and I stayed behind to joke around with the other guys and drink more beer.

Then, around 10 p.m. insanity struck, and I decided to find a dog for the kids. I staggered to my car, drove to a convenience store and bought a newspaper. Looking in the classifieds, I found a lady who wanted to find a home for a dog. I figured the kids would be happy with anything that barked and, before long, they'd forget all about Poor Dead Scruffy.

I dropped a dime in a pay phone and called the number in the paper and explained that I was doing a wonderful good deed, "...those poor, poor children have lost their dog..." and asked if I could come right away and pick him up. The lady was hesitant, but a little more pitiful talk on my behalf and she relented.

I showed up on her door step in about fifteen minutes and took possession of said dog. Oddly enough, he sort of resembled poor old Scruffy. It was dark.

I really didn't look at him that closely. He was sitting outside on the stoop when I arrived.

The lady didn't come out but spoke to me through the latched screen door. I thanked her, whisked the dog up and drove straight over to Swartz's mobile home. I knew Swartz didn't lock his doors at night.

I shut my ignition off before silently rolling to a stop in front of Swartz's place. I quietly opened the car door, gathered up the dog and crept up to Swartz's front door. It was dark inside. Swartz drank heavily and I knew he was dead to the world. I eased the door open with one hand and with the other shoved the dog inside and closed the door. I then headed back to the airport.

The next morning Swartz comes high-balling into the airport's dirt parking lot without the wife and kids. He hops out yelling at the top of his lungs, "Alright! Which one of you miserable assholes put that damn dog in my trailer last night?!"

We all just stood there looking sheepish and shrugged our shoulders. Trying to stifle a laugh at that moment was one the hardest things I ever did.

"That miserable little son-of-a-bitch has a bad case of fleas and he crapped all over my living room!" ranted Swartz pacing back-and-forth. "And to top that off, the kids were playing with him this morning when I got up and I think he's got the ringworm!!"

That did it. We all broke out laughing and holding our sides. We knew Swartz was in a pickle. He couldn't do anything in retaliation even if he knew who did it. Somebody might tell the kids what really happened to poor old Scruffy.

After a while, Swartz looked me dead in the face. He knew who had done it. After a few seconds of silence, he broke out laughing himself, twirled his bushy mustache a little and said, "Thanks anyway." We put our gear on and jumped the rest of the day.

A few months later, on a Saturday morning, we were all sitting around waiting on the weather to clear. Swartz's kids were chasing each other around the cars laughing and giggling. The new Scruffy had long since been freed of fleas and it turned out that there was no ringworm, after all.

Just then, a battered, red Ford pick-up rolled into the dusty parking lot and a tall, lanky, grizzled hulk of a man with a weather-beaten, craggy face got out of the truck and shuffled over towards us.

We figured he was just a local "whuffo" ("What fo ya'll jump out of dem 'planes?") coming to watch the action.

Turned out it was a local farmer. He walked up to Swartz and said, "Got a minute? I got sumpthin' in the truck I want to show ya." Swartz shook his head and followed the man back to his truck. I ambled along behind.

When we got to the truck, the man pointed in the bed and said, "Thought maybe you boys wud know sumpthin' about this." There, lying in the truck bed was Scruffy's harness. No dog. Just the harness attached to a still unopened parachute. Swartz's face turned three shades of white and he gulped. I started to chortle.

"Jest found it in the woods." Said the man. "Belong to ya'll?" Swartz was quick on his feet. Some color returned to his face as he glanced over his shoulder to see where his kids were. They were still running around the cars in an endless game of chase.

He thought for a minute then Swartz said, "Nope. Looks military to me. Maybe it fell out of one of the planes from Keesler?" The farmer thought about that for a minute and said, "Well, it had to fit somebody mighty small." With that, he spat a brown plug of chewing tobacco juice on the ground with a splat and he got in his truck and left.

Swartz's response? "Jesus. That was close."

I was laughing my ass off. And, it was the end of jumping with animals for Swartz. The whole episode reminded me of a time at Ft. Bragg when a bunch of guys decided to throw a chicken out the back of a C-130 just to see if chickens can fly.

They don't, by the way. And there's nothing left to fry afterwards.

Chapter Two

Southern Parachute Center & Leon

One day, I traveled to Mobile, Alabama, to a grand gathering of nearly every southern jumper at what was known as a Council Meeting. Mostly, it was a chance to renew old friendships and drink a lot of beer.

At the bar, where the meeting took place, I met Prissy. A willow of a girl, nearly anorexic, she stood at the bar wearing welding gloves and holding an ocelot. Ocelots have nasty tempers and very long, sharp claws. Also known as Dwarf Leopards, the ocelot resembles a large housecat and was once hunted to near extinction because of their beautiful silky spotted coats.

Prissy was easy to chat with and it came up that I was looking for work. "Well," she said, "we need somebody to train first jump students at the Center. But we can't pay much." I was such a gung-ho jumper, I said, "If you can give me a cot in a hanger, three meals a day and a little spending money, I'm there." Turns out, I would be there for four years. We agreed I would start in a few days. I was giddy with the prospects.

A few days later, when my Greyhound bus rolled into Hammond, Louisiana, where Southern Parachute Center was located, Prissy was waiting there waving and this time, without the snarling cat. I slung my parachute over my shoulder and stepped out into the humidity of summer. A short drive in a VW bug and we reached the airport, which was impressive.

The airport, it turned out, was one of many built during World War II. When the war was over, the airports were often sold or leased to the local municipalities for one dollar. Its primary purpose had been to train the pilots and crews of B-24 Liberator bombers which were used worldwide but, in the main, over Europe. It was the primary bomber used in the raids at Ploesti. Ploesti was the vast German oil refinery located some 30 miles north of Bucharest, Romania.

The airport had three five thousand foot concrete runways laid out in a massive triangle connected by taxiways. As I walked onto the apron of the airport, a figure emerged from the cockpit of a small red-and-white airplane. I would ultimately use that same aircraft to log over four thousand hours of pilot-in-command time. But that day, I wasn't yet a pilot. That was to come.

The figure materializing from the airplane was Leon, Prissy's husband, partner and the driving force behind the Center. Leon was Cajun. He had little education but a huge, gregarious personality and thrust his hand forward to shake mine flashing a smile full of teeth -- almost Cheshire-like.

"Mike!" he said, as he pumped my hand, "Come on in, I've heard good things about you." With that, he wheeled and starting walking towards the old airport terminal and lounge.

Once inside, I looked around at the walls and the green vinyl couches that lined the room. On every wall, there were old yellowed photos of ancient airplanes and a few newer pictures in black frames of various jumpers -- some I knew -- posing and grinning for the camera.

Hanging at the edges of the ceiling were many ragged pieces of colored cloth with hard-to-read writing on them like gay little flags. I pointed and asked, "What are those?"

"Oh!" said Leon, "In addition to skydiving, we also do flight instruction. Those are shirttails."

He went on, "When we solo a new student pilot, he has to have his shirttail cut off. We then write his name and the date of his solo flight on them and hang them there. It's an old flying custom." To this day, I have never taken the time to find out where it originated. Mine would eventually hang there as well.

Leon, it would turn out, would prove himself to be a true one-of-a-kind. He spoke with a slight, very slight, Cajun accent that could disappear when he needed to speak with someone and he really wanted to impress them with his education. But he wasn't educated.

He never got out of junior high from what I can tell. Yet, he was an idiot savant in many ways -- 'mechanically gifted' is a misnomer. Everything mechanical came to him easily, as if he had the entire Encyclopedia of Mechanics in his head. Nothing existed he could not fix, somehow. I do not know who taught him to fly, but it had to have been easy to do. He was a natural pilot.

Over the course of the years, I learned how to fly from him. His way of teaching me how to fly is best illustrated by this small example.

We had three airplanes at the Center. Two of them were used to haul jumpers. The first, the one I spent the most time flying, was a four place Cessna 170, a tail dragger. Meaning, it had a tail wheel rather than a nose gear.

The second was a Howard GDA-15P, a heavy six-place airplane -- a beast produced in the 1930s as an air ambulance and instrument trainer. Also a tail dragger, from the pilot's seat you could not see over the nose, meaning you had to constantly be looking askew out the side windows to taxi. It was very tricky to taxi, take off and land.

The Howard's engine was a Pratt and Whitney R985, very powerful at 450 horsepower. The engine was hard to start, and when it did, it belched fire and blew large clouds of gray-bluish smoke out behind it. This airplane was a scary animal to me as a new pilot. It had very touchy brakes. Stomp on them a little too hard and the airplane would flip straight over onto its back.

It carried nearly 100 gallons of fuel in the belly tanks which you were literally sitting on top of. Landing it, to me, was a prayerful occasion. For a time, in the beginning, I was truly afraid it was going to kill me. I'd have nightmares about it.

But we needed it because it could carry as many as six jumpers as opposed to the 170 which could only carry three. It simply made more money. We charged jumpers by the altitude they wanted to go to -- the higher the altitude, the more free fall time. The Howard could also get them there much, much faster than the 170 which we mostly used for the students who jumped at lower altitudes.

The way Leon taught me to fly the Howard was simple in design. One day, just after I had received my Private Pilot's license, which, in those days, only required 40 hours of flight time, he came strolling out of the hanger and said, "Hey, Whip!" That was his nickname for me along with "Hotrod."

"Jerk the engine cover off of the Howard. We're gonna go play around."

He had previously given me some flight instruction in it over the course of about two hours of flying time. I had barely figured out what I was doing with it. I thought, *"Okay, more instruction."* As we approached the airplane he said, "You take the yoke." "Yoke" being the flight controls.

That meant I was going to be in the pilot's seat -- flying. I shuddered.

I really didn't feel ready yet and I was always on the verge of wetting my pants at the prospect of flying the Howard. The airplane I flew the most, the 170, I could handle very well.

He took the co-pilot's seat, the right seat, which really wasn't a seat. It was the frame the right seat was supposed to be mounted on. But that seat had been taken off the frame to accommodate more jumpers. So, he wasn't belted in. The belts went with the seat. He was just perched there, sitting next me on the right seat's mounting frame, grinning

Now, our pilot's seats in both airplanes always had an emergency parachute sitting in them, which we never put on unless we should need it, if say, a wing fell off. We just sat in the seat and used the parachute as a back cushion. We could always slip right into it, if we needed it, which we never did.

He then motioned to me to fire up the engine. I primed it several times, flipped the magnetos on and hit the starter button. The big engine barked a few times and it caught. With much blue smoke belching from its exhaust stack and the smell of burned fuel filling the cockpit, I watched as the various instruments flickered and came to life.

We sat there warming it up for a few minutes then Leon motioned to me to taxi out. So, I swallowed hard and pushed the throttle forward and tried to look brave. He was sitting there, and out of the corner of my eye, I could see he was flashing me the Cheshire grin, teeth and all.

I strained to see what little I could ahead as we rolled towards the runaway and the threshold. Once at the threshold, the start of the runway, I positioned the Howard for take-off, locked the brakes and brought the engine rpm up to do oil pressure and magneto checks.

That all looked good and with some hesitation I pushed the throttle full forward and released the brakes. A little way down the runway, the airspeed was coming up nicely and the tail lifted and I could see the horizon again. Breathing a small sigh of relief, I glanced at the airspeed and I eased the yoke back and we lifted off gently.

We were airborne, and I knew, at least, temporarily, the monster wasn't going to kill me yet. Flying it straight and level wasn't the problem. Leon instructed me to circle the airport at about two thousand feet. I was getting more comfortable now and leaned back some trying to just enjoy the flight.

After I reached altitude and circled the airport two or three times, Leon got right up in my face and yelled, "Lean forward." I did, without question. I usually did everything Leon told me to without question.

The next thing I know he has snatched the emergency rig out from behind me and he's putting it on. Now, he's leaning out the open door with his left hand in the air holding up two fingers and pointing left which means "Give me 10 degrees left rudder."

"Oh, Christ!," I thought, screaming in my head, *"He's getting out!"* I was right, and with a whoosh, he was gone and I was alone with the killer airplane. I was going to have to land it. There was no way around it. It was land it right or die. Period.

Leon would later tell me that he had known I had an unreasonable fear of the Howard. He figured that the best way to teach me to swim was just throw me in water and let things take their course. He also knew that I was a very good pilot and that I had just built the Howard up in my mind to be such a problem that if I didn't conquer it on my own, I was never going to get past it. So, he had given me the problem – I had to fix it.

I circled the airport once or twice more and started figuring to myself that he wouldn't have done that if he thought he was going to lose a pilot and one of his two primary income sources. We weren't rich, and over the four years I was there, we always lived hand-to-mouth. I took some comfort in that and eased the throttle back to descend.

I took my time. I did everything by the book. I started talking to myself. *"Power setting, right! Check airspeed. Flaps to slow the descent and speed, right! Fuel selector on the correct tank, right! Check airspeed again."*

I wiped my hands on my pants leg several times and took a firm grip on the yoke and placed my hand perfectly on the throttle and checked my airspeed once more. The runway, all 5000 glimmering feet of it was stretched out ahead of me. Just as began my flare for the landing, out of the corner of my eye, I spied Leon squatting the high grass watching.

I went past him, and my wheels touched down on the runway with a two quick screeches. I rolled out to the end of the runway, swerving a little here and there, as the tail wheel lowered to the concrete. I had landed with little difficulty. I exhaled deeply and sat back some in the seat.

Once at the end of the runway, I gave her some throttle, leaned on one brake and spun her back in Leon's direction at the other end of the runway. I had landed the Howard solo with no help from anybody, and there was a huge smile on my face.

I taxied to the runway's end. Once there, I slowed, then stopped and Leon crawled in with his parachute bundled in his arms and he sat down on the floor in the back of the cabin. We didn't say anything. He was just giving me the Cheshire grin. There was nothing to say. I wasn't mad at him, just happy for me.

This was just beginning of an extraordinary education in many things at his hands.

Chapter Three

The Bumper Sticker Debacle

Leon was the central figure at Southern Parachute Center.

He had started jumping there as a student and before long had gotten his pilot's license. Later in life, he would have many licenses for doing numerous different things, ranging from flight instructor to parachute rigger to tug boat captain, just to name a few. Much later in life he, somehow or another, became an itinerant preacher.

In the mid-sixties, he had fallen in love with sport parachuting and with Prissy who was a fellow student jumper. The Center, its airplanes and all the parachute gear had come up for sale. He went to his mother, a flamboyant and eccentric woman, a collector of carousel horses, and he borrowed the down payment from her.

I came to know Cajuns pretty well living in south Louisiana. In many ways, as a Cajun, Leon was typical. Most of them are friendly, sociable and charitable folks – as was Leon.

Leon had a restless and brilliant mind, always finding ways to do big things with few resources. Many times, that involved leaning on the good graces of others to help him to accomplish big jobs with little reward to his benefactors. Most of the time, when he was around, you could almost hear Zydeco music. He was a pretty cheerful guy.

A born teacher, one of the first things he taught me was humility. I was brash and loud-mouthed and very certain of everything I said, and I would stand on it as absolute fact even in face of overwhelming evidence to the contrary.

Often, I was wrong in what I would say, and I would have to apologize later. The first lesson he taught me was to preface everything I said that I had the least little doubt about with "I could be wrong, but..." To this day, it's a primary phrase in my language.

In those times, Leon, Prissy and myself were together most of everyday. Occasionally, Prissy would need to take some part-time job in order to help us make ends meet, which never quite did. But, unless we were in our respective beds, in my case, an old fold-out couch in the hanger, Leon and I were always together and became a close-knit team.

My role in the beginning was teaching students that we charged $25, how to make their first jumps. His role in that was flying the airplane. These roles would become interchangeable later on.

The bond showed itself most often when we were running jump operations with him as pilot and me as jumpmaster -- or vice-versa. Few words needed to be spoken between us. In those days, I was all wild hare and he was all "older, wiser brother." The roles would reverse later – drastically. But back then, if he said, "Let's do this or that...," I was very much the soldier and followed orders.

Leon was made of rubber mixed with steel. In Louisiana, especially during the spring, the weather would be tumultuous and fronts with black low hanging clouds raced through from west to east for weeks at a time. Very little jumping took place for days on end.

The airplanes sat idle and we looked for ways to occupy ourselves. One week-end, the rain fell endlessly with few breaks and water ponded on the low spots on the runways. Runway 24-6 in particular had a virtual lake in the middle of it that was quite large. The winds blew at high speeds constantly.

He came into the rigging loft where we packed and maintained our parachutes one rainy, windy Saturday morning with a water ski tucked under one arm – a Slalom water ski. It was designed so that a skier only used the single water ski and it had two foot cups on it. Wider than a regular water ski, it had a flat bottom and no rudder.

Other jumpers and I had gathered in there, drinking coffee while we prayed and hoped the weather was going clear enough that we could get a load up. He then announced, matter-of-factly, "I'm going water skiing." We all looked at him like he had forks sticking in his eyes.

He walked over to the parachute rack and grabbed the oldest, rattiest rig we owned and threw it over his shoulder. "Com'on. It'll be fun!" On the way out he looked behind the door and picked up a short length of iron pipe leaning against the wall. We fell in line behind him without question, and along we went.

We all knew that if he thought something up, an event was going to happen we wouldn't want to miss.

So off we marched, through the rain, following him like the Pied Piper across the expansive airport to the runway where the most extensive of the ponding had taken place. Once there, he tells several guys to open the parachute, disconnect it from the harness and lay the canopy out, which was no easy affair with the wind gusting up to 40 miles an hour.

Then he takes the piece of pipe and slides it into the risers. Risers are the nylon straps at the end of the canopy lines that attach to the harness itself. What he has now vaguely resembles a kind of ski tow rope with the pipe being the handle the skier holds on to and the parachute lines that would be the ski rope. He then slips the ski on his feet and hollers at the guys to hold the canopy open.

He had previously checked the wind direction to ensure it would take him skiing across the large pond on the runway. The plan was to allow the wind to fill the parachute and the parachute would pull him across to the other side. I think we all secretly knew this would not end well.

Just as the guys held the canopy off the ground to expose it to the wind, the wind shifted forty degrees off to the side of the runway and doubled in speed.

The canopy opened with a "WHUMP!" and Leon was completely airborne at first, then it dashed him, hard, to the ground. Then he was airborne once again; then, it slammed him to the ground again. He wouldn't let go of the pipe. This happened a third time and the wind took him to about 15 feet off the ground and slammed him down once more.

He let go that time and lay there on his back for a few seconds. Then popped right to his feet flashing the Cheshire grin we'd all come to expect as if to say "Ta-Da!" He was laughing, a high pitched, "Heh-heh-heh!" A lesser man would have had multiple broken bones. Not him. Like I said, "rubber and steel."

On another occasion, he was brooding all day. "What's the matter?" I asked.

"We're gonna lose the airport and have to shut down." He said gloomily. "What do you mean?" I said. "Well, you know that damn city councilman, the one that thinks we're just a bunch of hippies fallin' out of airplanes?" I nodded yes.

"Well," Leon said, "he's running for re-election, and has said that if he wins, he's gonna close us down and turn the airport into an industrial park." Actually that is exactly what happened years later.

I could see Leon was hatching a plan. Sometimes his plotting worked in our favor, other times, not so much. We didn't say much more about it and I got busy packing parachutes. He left for the day.

A few days later, he comes into the loft wearing a beaming smile. In his arms, he's carrying a box. He says, "Look what I got. I had 'em printed up in Amite." Amite was a small town north of Hammond.

I peered into the box. Stacked inside the box were hundreds of bumper stickers that said "Vote for So & So" the despised city councilman. I looked at Leon with a *"What the hell...?"* look on my face.

"You know what we're gonna do?" Now, did you get the "we're" part? I had been recruited and this was Leon and he knew I was a loyal soldier. "No. What?" I said.

"Well..." he says, "...we're gonna get us a few gallons of shellac and sneak around town tonight shellacking these to car windshields right in front of the driver's seat." I snickered because I had no sense at all in those days, and because I had never been in jail yet, and I didn't know how monotonous a diet of baloney sandwiches and Kool-Aid could be. I said, "We're gonna need lots of beer." He agreed.

Leon had also recruited Herbie to help. I protested. To me, that was asking to get caught as Herbie could screw up a wet dream, but Leon was insistent that Herbie help out and I relented. So Herbie showed up and we sat around drinking beer until almost midnight.

Once we were sure that Hammond had pretty well gone to bed, we jumped in the truck and headed to town. Once in town, we sought out one neighborhood after another and spent hours creeping around in the dark, first slathering a swath of shellac across windshields and then slapping a sticker in the right spot.

Now, Leon's reason for this was simple. The townsfolk would figure that Mr. Hated Councilman had hired somebody to distribute his bumper stickers and they had gotten drunk and stupidly affixed them to the windshields in a bumbling way hoping to get the driver's attention. In fact, Leon was going to make sure Mister Councilman was going to be blamed.

The voters, therefore, would then conclude Mr. Councilman was a dumbass and they would not reelect him. To Leon, it was the perfect plan. That is until the gendarmes showed up.

While we were up on somebody's dark carport with Leon slathering and me affixing, Herbie whispered loudly and insistently, "Cops!"

Just then, a street over, somebody started cussing loudly about his windshield. We had been discovered. The black-and-white police car rolled silently by without spotting us and we hauled tail in the other direction leaving our shellac bucket and brush behind.

After running a short distance, Leon whispered, "Split up!" And we did. I took a dark path back towards the center of town where Leon's house was at the time, figuring to meet him there later. Dashing through backyards in the pitch black of a moonless night was dangerous. I nearly hung myself on two clotheslines and slammed my shin against what I could only figure to be one of those sprinkler pipes used to water lawns.

Out-of-breath, I made it back to Leon's house and snuck in the backdoor. I knew Prissy would be upstairs asleep -- but not for long. The phone rang. I was standing in the kitchen getting ready to head out the door and take off when Prissy turned the light on upstairs lighting up the stairway. I waited in the dark kitchen breathlessly.

She came down the stairs cussing under her breath and turned on the living room light then picked up the phone. "Hello?"

"What! WHAT?! What'd he do?"

"Malicious vandalism!"

"Bond is how much!?"

"I'll be right there!"

I stood tight in the kitchen and didn't make a sound. Prissy slammed the phone down and ran upstairs to get dressed. As she raced up the stairs, I snuck out the screen door and made my way back to the airport and the couch.

Most mornings, when Leon arrived at the airport, he was carrying a coffee for me and himself when he got out of the truck. Normally, he didn't smile a whole lot until the coffee kicked in an hour or so later. But, the morning after our little crusade and his and Herbie's arrest, he was all smiles. I looked at him and said, "What in the world's got you so happy?"

"We got thrown in the pokey last night!"

"I heard." I said . "I still don't get it. Why are you happy about that? And, by the way, I got away. How come you didn't?"

He thought about that a second and said, "Well, actually Herbie got caught. I didn't -- not at first."

"What do you mean?"

"Well, I was hiding down the street in the woods when they caught Herbie and I wanted to have a little fun. So, I popped out of the woods and started walking down the street towards them. They had Herbie in handcuffs and were about to put him in the squad car. I just walked by nonchalantly and said, "Evening!" The cops just turned and looked at me."

"Yeah," I said. "what happened then?"

"Well, just as I walked by them, one of the cops hollered, "Come back here!" So, I turned and went back."

I waited for the rest of the story.

"When I walked up to them, one of the cops spun me around and there was a bumper sticker stuck to my ass."

I am now roaring with laughter.

"Prissy bonded us out and the court date's next month."

"But why are you so happy about it."

"Cause." He said with a straight face. "When we show up in front of the judge, he's going to ask me why we did this. Then, I'm going to say that Mr. Councilman paid us to put out the bumper stickers."

Sure enough, when the trial came up, Leon was standing in front of the judge. The Councilman had shown up and was sitting in the back of the courtroom, gloating, I suppose, because Leon was in trouble. The judge proceeded to ask Leon what possessed him to do what he did. Without hesitation, Leon turned and pointed at the Councilman and said in a very calm voice, "He paid us to do it!"

The Councilman tried to sneak out of the courtroom but the judge ordered him to stay. Then it became Leon's word against the Councilman's insistence it was a lie. But it was too late. Everyone in the room had heard enough to start passing rumors around town.

In the end, Leon and Herbie got no jail time and short probations and the nasty old Councilman wasn't reelected.

We would be at that airport for some time to come. Politics is a dirty business.

Chapter Four

Cardinal Puff

Most of our jumpers came in from places like Baton Rouge or Mobile and some as far away as Europe. Occasionally floating through were members of the U.S. Army Parachute Team, the "Golden Knights."

Nearly every week-end, we had several people overnight in tents or on the floor at my apartment. (I had moved up in the world.) Some stayed for weeks at a time. New Orleans was only about 60 miles away and it was as much an attraction for some of them as the jumping.

We kept the prices for jump tickets, an aircraft boarding pass, as cheap as possible, and that was another attraction for them. I usually got to the airport early in the morning and was never surprised to find somebody sleeping in their car or balled up on the ground in a sleeping bag. There were always new people coming to jump and life was full of surprises.

But no surprise was one activity that took place at the Center along with the jumping – partying. We had a hard and fast rule, however.

No alcohol during the day while jump operations were going on. But when jumping was done for the day, coolers popped open. Things could get crazy after that.

Jumpers aren't your usual party people. Most of them, not all are classic risk takers and the old saw, "Here, honey, hold my beer -- watch this..." was in frequent use.

Now, we weren't your typical drinkers. We were noble drinkers with distinct classes within our small society. One could always choose to opt out of the class structure we had established. But you were considered cowardly in some way if you never made the attempt to enter. Not that anyone ever said anything to you.

We merely allowed you to hover on the fringes and suffer in your own pangs of remorse at not having tried to gain the rank. When you did ask to be considered for membership, you had to do so formally. This is how it worked.

You would approach a jumper who had successfully passed the ritual's demands, such as a ranking Cardinal or a Cardinal Supreme, a Bishop, or better yet, a Pope. Then, in all humility, you would ask words to the effect,

"May I become a Cardinal, sir?" If granted an attempt, your initiation would begin.

You would take a seat at a table across from the ranking Cardinal. In a very high and ceremonious fashion, he would lean across the table and fill a glass to the brim with beer.

You would then be shown, once, the following demonstration and would then be expected to repeat it yourself making not one mistake, no matter how small. There could be no spillage of beer whatsoever. Once finished with a successful attempt, your glass would be tipped upside down. You were allowed not one remaining drop.

During the ceremony, you would have to perform this:

Hold the glass at the rim with your thumb and forefinger and hoist it outwards, saying, "I drink to the honorable Cardinal Puff for the first time tonight." Then consume what you can but not the whole glass. You will have to make five more swallows from what is left. Then, tap the glass, once on the tabletop, and set it down.

Then, with the forefinger of each hand, tap the tabletop alternating left and right, then tap the underside of the tabletop, tap each thigh top, stomp each foot, stand up, then sit down once.

Then grab the glass again, hoist it aloft using the thumb, index and forefinger and toast, "To the Cardinal Puff Puff, for the second time this evening." Then drink two more swallows, tap the glass twice on the table top, then use two fingers and repeat the first step (tap, tap, etc...)

On the third try, you will say, "I drink to the Cardinal Puff, Puff, Puff, for the third and final time this evening." Hoist the glass using your thumb, and three fingers and consume the rest of the remaining brew in three separate drinks making sure there is none left in the glass. With three fingers, repeat the tapping sequence (three times each, obviously). Upon finishing the tapping sequence and the sitting sequence, you take the glass with an inverted grip and proclaim "Once a Cardinal, always a Cardinal, never spill a drop."

While proclaiming this, you invert the glass, release your grip and then invert (to upright) again. There should be no liquid from the glass on the tabletop from the inverted glass. If there is, you repeat the whole process again!

If there is none, the ruling Cardinal will ask you, "Are you a Cardinal?" To which you shall reply, "You bet your sweet ass I am!" Any other answer is unacceptable and results in having to repeat the whole process again.

Then in the future, if you are approached and asked "Are you a Cardinal?" The only answer can be, "You bet your sweet ass I am." The person asking the question may then challenge you by saying, "Prove it." The person asking must be a Cardinal and prove they are by performing the ritual before you do.

The basic level is Cardinal Puff, accomplished by using one large glass of beer. To become a Bishop requires two full glasses of beer; the first glass is fully consumed on round one, then parts two and three on glass two. Arch Bishop takes three full glasses, one for each part of the game. Pope requires a pitcher. In order to proceed up the ranks, you have to accomplish each rank ritual before it at one sitting!

Now as one might imagine, this ceremony requires high volumes of alcohol. But we did not do this every time we gathered.

It was only those times that an uninitiated lurker hovering on the fringes of our Cardinal Puff aristocracy screwed up his courage and asked that the ritual be demonstrated, that the beer flowed in such quantities.

Now, each Cardinal Puff or higher rank giving a demonstration had his own moral standards when overseeing a new initiate attempting to perform the sacrament. An applicant could be "called" for anything large or small in detail, be it the manner in which they held the glass or sat in their chair. But, usually, applicants would quickly defeat themselves with a misstep in movements, whether it be missing a series of taps, or not standing then sitting when appropriate.

When mistakes were made, judgment was swift. And the sentence was always the same: hang the glass to your lips and immediately drink the entire contents and keep the glass suspended at the lips until only "dust" remained or you were given permission to remove it.

This is where the real merriment began, for the drunker one became, the harder it was to perform the complexities of the game and the more one failed, the more one wanted to pass.

So more drinking would ensue, insuring that nearly everyone involved would, sooner or later, pass out.

Somewhere in there, between the beginnings of the victim attempting to pass the test multiple times and the passing out came high, loud stages of drunkenness and new games would start to be invented that usually had something to do with elevated states of bravado caused by elevated amounts of alcohol.

Two come to mind. The first was Light Socket Cardinal. The other was Dead Ant.

Light Socket Cardinal was a pure game of dangerous dare. It required one to be too drunk to think rationally. It was quite simple. The applicant would have to ask for a ritual. Usually that was in the form of a highly slurred request, as in, "Shur? Wanna show it to me?" Now, by this time, the individual giving the demo was simply being invited to stick a finger in an empty light socket as a demonstration. Everybody already knew what this game was about.

Either the socket would be electrified or not. I only ever saw one guy take the challenge and he didn't know that the lamp was unplugged but he did it anyway.

The challenger was already too drunk to see it and they argued about it the entire next day as to whether or the guying performing the challenge actually did it.

The next level of drunken gamesmanship, Dead Ant, had to take place at a bar with several inebriated jumpers sitting on barstools late at night just before the bar was due to close. I saw this game played many times resulting in several concussions.

The guys would all be sitting at the bar, chatting up girls or discussing all things parachuting or telling war stories when someone suddenly called out "DEAD ANT!"

On that command, you were to push immediately, straight back as hard as you could, and land flat on your back with your arms and legs sticking up in the air. The last man down had to buy the next round.

The beauty of it was that no one hollered "Dead Ant" until much later at night when everyone was already so drunk that a fall like that didn't bother you much. But, once in a while, you'd hear the crack of somebody's skull slapping the floor.

Light Socket Cardinal and Dead Ant were the truest of "Here, honey, hold my beer -- watch this." moments.

Chapter Five

The Gloom Fear

Saturday and Sunday mornings would bring us college students, professionals and regular folks all bent on becoming sky-gods. Then, they would plunk down their cash and spend the next three hours locked away in a classroom and then move outside on specially built equipment. There, I would teach them the intricacies of how parachutes worked, how to handle a parachute that decides not to open, how to land, how to steer, how to exit, and many things they would need to know. Things they would immediately forget as soon as they put the parachute on to go up the first time.

One of those students was especially memorable because he became the only one I ever refused to let jump.

In those days, over the course of the years, I trained well over 1,000 first jump students. I can honestly say that only a few of those were cognizant of their surroundings and thinking clearly as they left the airplane on their first jump.

The rest were operating from rote memory, and because I was pointing out every next move they needed to make. The worst one who leaps to mind was a gentleman who went through my class and, as I trained him, I felt he was clear-headed and fearless -- or at least, had his fear under control.

My habit, after making sure a student's equipment was in order, immediately prior to making a first jump, was to sit in the back seat of the airplane right next to the open door. Then I would have the first student out sit on the floor between my legs so that when the time came to exit, they could simply swing their legs out and let them dangle in the air.

The second student to jump was positioned on the back seat next to me to my left. In that position, I could also keep both hands on the shoulders of the student getting ready to go as a sort of comfort to them.

That also served to make sure that if there was an in-flight emergency, I could easily toss them out of the airplane. In addition, it made it easier to communicate with them, as all I had to do was to lean forward and yell in their ear.

I don't remember this gentleman's name but I do recall that he when he went through training, he didn't show me the kind of fear that would make me suspect that he would freeze or panic. I usually had a very good eye for spotting potential problems with students.

After his three hours of ground training in the classrooms, then learning to exit, learning how to arch his back to fall away stable, and making mock parachute landing falls, I thought him ready. After lunch, it was time to jump. I helped him get his gear on and checked that everything was in good order. He seemed confident and had few questions.

We made our way to the idling airplane where Leon was leaning out watching to see that no one banged their head on the wing. I put the gentleman in the seat next to me on the left side. I put a second student, who would be first out, on the floor between my legs. Leon looked back to see that all was in order and I gave him a thumbs up. We began to taxi and soon reached the runway and Leon gave it full throttle. The little Cessna rolled down the runway, the tail lifted and we were airborne. After circling the airport a few times while climbing to the standard jump altitude of 2,500 feet, we turned in on jump run.

Once at altitude, I leaned out the door to check our flight path, I gave Leon a few heading corrections, yelled at the student between my legs to swing his legs out. Then once I was sure of our position over the ground, I told the first student to "Stand on the step!" -- that is to put his feet on a special step built over the main gear and take a position leaning forward with his hands gripping the airplane's wing strut.

Once over the jump "spot," I would slap them on their rear end and yell, "Go!" The student would loosen his grip and push off backwards. After a very short fall, a static line would break open the holding closure on their parachute pack and pull out the parachute which would, hopefully, billow out behind them and open. I never once had a student parachute malfunction.

Now, the second student, the gentleman, had been watching all of this, and I suppose he had built up a case of what we called the "gloom fear" – an unreasonable horror had settled in his mind that he would fall to his death, or his parachute wasn't going to open. They had a spare parachute called a "reserve" that they could open in case their main parachutes malfunctioned.

The "gloom fear" is an insidious thing, and I've seen jumpers succumb to it many times. It can set in after being newly married or having children or seeing someone else get hurt or "bounce" – that is to die – and sometimes it's short lived -- sometimes it is not.

One jumper I knew got a case of the gloom fear so bad after a near accident that he went to his car, gathered up a lot of very expensive parachute gear, walked back to our office, dumped it all on the floor, said "I quit." Then he turned and left. We never saw him again. It was good gear. We enjoyed using it afterwards.

As soon as the first student jumped, I watched him long enough to see that his parachute had opened properly, which it did. He was on own now. Leon banked to the right and began a turn to bring us back around. As Leon rolled out level to repeat the jump run, I turned my attention to the gentleman. I hooked up his static line and moved him into the position on the floor between my legs. Afterwards, leaning over his shoulder, looking out the door, I started checking our flight path again.

Without looking at him, using my left hand, I gave Leon a flight path correction and once he made the correction, I turned back in the gentleman's direction. As I did so, Leon got my attention by pointing at the gentleman. Leon's eyes were a big as quarters. He was motioning for me to look at the gentleman's face.

I leaned forward and looked into his face which was stone rigid, his lips were pursed, his jaws were tight and he had bruising around his eyes just as if he'd been in a fight. The blood vessels around his eyes had burst. He was completely terrified. His respiration was rapid and he was breathing in fast wheezes. I could not let him jump in that condition. His mind had shut down.

I then got worried he might actually fall out the aircraft unintentionally. In that case, he would not have had the presence of mind to do anything but fall if his main canopy had a problem opening. I wrapped my arms completely around him in a bear hug and began giving him assurances in the most soothing tone I could muster that he didn't have to jump and that we were returning to the airport.

Leon and I had spent so many hours in the air together over the years that I didn't have to tell him to land. He was already descending and lining up on the runway.

I maintained my hug on the gentleman right up until the time that Leon shut the engine down. Leon unbuckled his seat belt, crawled over the gentleman and hopped out. He then turned and started helping me ease the guy out to the ground.

He could barely walk, he was so frozen. We escorted him over to a bench, shucked his gear off of him and sat him down. In a few minutes, after a few swigs of water, his breathing started to return to normal and the color began returning to his face. His face, around his eyes, would remain bruised and bluish. A crowd of jumpers gathered around trying to see what had happened.

He had not said one word in the airplane or for a long time after we took him to the bench. But I could see him thinking. Shortly, he spoke saying "I'm really sorry, everybody."

Over the course of having trained hundreds of successful students, many of whom had returned to continue jumping with us, we just didn't know what to say to him. I fumbled for words. "Look, sir," I said, "We have never made anybody jump and never will." Leon nodded in agreement. "We just want you to have fun, and frankly, we'd rather not let anybody jump that doesn't completely want to." That seemed to settle him down some.

Then I lied, "Everybody freezes up once in a while." Leon knew what I was doing and again nodded in agreement. This guy was my student and Leon knew to let me handle things. I reached out and put my hand on the gentleman's shoulder and said, "We're going to give you back your money. It's fine, don't worry." The gentleman looked me in the face and said, "After I settle down, can I come back and try again?"

I looked him straight in the face, glanced at Leon and turned back to the gentleman and said, "No. Take up golf."

We never saw him again. I keep looking for him to show up on a PGA tour.

Chapter Six

Eddie and the Body

The decision was made that I had served enough time sleeping on the fold-out couch, and Leon starting paying me enough to find a place to live. I found an apartment in town.

I had a roommate, Eddie. He was the manager of a local backwater FM station. I had met him when I called in an entry in a record give-a-way. We became great friends, and I'm still in touch with him today.

I lost track of him for a while when he took a job at another radio station in upstate Mississippi. When I finally relocated him many years later, he had somehow pulled himself together, gone back to school, gotten his CPA and is now a senior partner in an accounting firm in Baton Rouge.

When I got him on the phone and asked him what motivated him to get his CPA, he said that he had taken up heavy drinking and slid steadily into an alcoholic's abyss. His wake up call came when he awoke one morning to find a one-legged woman hobbling around his kitchen making squirrel stew.

She said they had married during the night, but neither could remember the other's name. He stopped drinking right then and there, moved back home to Louisiana, enrolled in college, and got his degree. Currently, he is married, has a big family and is doing very well for himself.

Before all that happened, Eddie and I were having a high old time being footloose bachelors in Hammond.

There came the time that everybody, Leon, Prissy, and everybody else, had gone to compete in the National Parachuting Championships in Tahlequah, Oklahoma, and I was left to man the phones and to fly the occasional jumper who drifted by.

One day, the phone rang. It was a funeral home in New Orleans who asked if I'd be willing to fly up to Memphis, pick up a body and fly it back to New Orleans. "You betcha!" I answered. We were all starving and nearly broke. I would agree to fly anything but drugs to make money. I got the rest of the instructions from the funeral home and hung up.

A plan hatched!

Eddie was always bugging me to fly him somewhere for fun. He had made one jump but had never flown anywhere far away.

I picked up the phone and called Eddie at the radio station. "Hey, man! I just got a call from a guy who wants me to fly up to Memphis and pick up his two daughters who are going to college up there. "Wanna tag along?" "Be there in fifteen minutes!" he responded and hung up with a loud click.

Eddie and I were about the same age. We loved chasing women and drinking beer. Strange things were always happening. One night, when I got home, I couldn't find him and figured he was out on a date or something.

Then I heard him yelling outside. I looked out the window. Our apartment was on the second floor overlooking a Shell gas station. We often sat out on the station roof and watched the world go by. On its roof, the station had a rotating, lit, big yellow Shell sign which was perched up on a twenty foot steel pole.

And, there was Eddie, sitting atop the sign as it rotated round and round riding it like a horse. Every time he rotated towards the police station across the street, he would flip them off with both hands and holler obscenities. He was drunk as shit. The cops came out looked at him, shook their heads and walked back in the station.

One night, I had a date in Baton Rouge but didn't have a car. Eddie allowed me to borrow his car to make the trip. I got all dressed up in my best Nehru shirt and suit (Yeah, it was the 60's.) and tucked my two shot derringer in my pocket and hit the road.

Along the way, for some reason, I took the derringer out and slid it into the arm rest opening that stuck out from the driver's door. It just fit in the opening. A little later, I accidentally leaned on it with my elbow. It slipped through the arm rest, cocking itself as it fell and hit floor. Blam! It fired on impact with the floor. The bullet ricocheted off the bottom of the steel dash and splattered all over the tops of my feet.

The next morning, when I came limping back in, Eddie wanted know what happened to me. I told him I shot his car. He just shrugged and went back to his Corn Pops.

On the side of the road, where I had pulled over to examine my feet and hop around screaming a lot, I threw the damn gun into the woods and never carried anything with an exposed hammer again except in the military. The damage wasn't permanent as the derringer was a .22 caliber. Eddy figured stranger things had happened to us and this incident wasn't worth getting upset over.

Back at the parachute center, Eddie came barreling around the corner and jumped out of his car, shaving kit in hand, almost before the car had come to a stop.

Prior to Eddie's arrival I had gone out to the 170 and removed the back seat. When we got to Nashville, I would take out Eddie's seat, the co-pilot's seat, and place it behind mine. I would also remove the right door and load the funeral home stretcher over the wing struts and place it on the open space of the cabin alongside Eddie and myself.

My plan was to load it so the body's head would be to the rear, adjacent to Eddie. The weather was deteriorating quickly and I told Eddie to jump in. Once in the airplane, Eddie wanted to know where the back seat was. "Oh!" I said, "The girls will have a lot of baggage, they can sit on top of it." That satisfied him and I shoved the throttle forward and we took off.

En route, the weather had really soured, so much so that at one point I had slid over the Mississippi river to get below the cloud deck and navigated northward following the river.

At times we were at tree top height. Eddie was nervous. At one point, about midway, I had to land at Vicksburg due to low fuel and the bad weather. The weather was so bad, we decided to overnight. I slipped away from Eddie and called Memphis and told them we'd be there in the morning. He was still none-the-wiser.

The next morning we landed at Memphis. While taxing in, I told Eddie to jump out at the small terminal and go get us an egg sandwich and also told him that I was going to taxi to the other side of the airport and load up the girls.

Where I was going, Eddie couldn't see. As he got out, I also asked him to also bring me a carton of chocolate milk. I then taxied around the corner and found the waiting hearse. The funeral home guys helped me load the body in the airplane. The picture is, I'm left front seat, Eddie will sit behind me. The stretcher with the body, a female covered with a purple funeral home blanket, will lie along the entire length of the right side of the cabin.

I put the cabin door back on and taxied around to where Eddie was waiting with the egg sandwiches.

I almost couldn't contain myself as Eddie ran up to the cabin and opened the door. When he looked inside, his face turned two shades of white and he jumped back a foot or so and dropped the bag with the sandwiches.

"Where the hell are the girls!?!" he hollered over the engine noise. "Oh! I said, "One of 'em ain't coming and this one's not feeling so good. So, we're just taking her home." He was now frozen in place. "Come on. Get in. She ain't gonna bother you, I promise." Little did he know.

He just stood there shaking his head for a second or two, then he flipped me the bird, picked up the bag and crawled over her and sat down. "Where's my sandwich?" I asked. He silently handed me the sandwich and the chocolate milk. I put the wrapped sandwich in my lap. I would eat it en route.

I took the milk carton and placed it between the body's feet so it wouldn't fall over. I heard Eddy gasp over the sound of the engine. I had an ear-to-ear grin on my face.

This was going to be a hilarious show.

I *knew* Eddie had an unreasonable fear of death. He was now silent as he could be and was huddled all the way against the cabin wall with his face almost pressed against the window while looking over his shoulder at the outline beneath the stretcher blanket. "Relax!" I hollered, "Sit back and enjoy the ride." He didn't. I was now climbing for as much altitude as I could get. "Why" in a minute.

Here is what Eddie didn't know. When an airplane with a dead body in it climbs, the un-embalmed corpse will start to do funny things. They will belch, pass wind and twitch. Not in any necessary order. If they're in a casket, you'll never know. But merely laid out on a stretcher with a funeral home blanket spread over them, some of the movements can be quite visible. The first time it happens to you, it will raise the hair on the back of your neck. And I was climbing not only to see the show that was about to unfold, but for another reason as well. I was going to put the airplane on the step.

By climbing to a much higher altitude, you can then trim the bird to slightly lose altitude over a very long distance thereby using less throttle than you would normally have to use to cruise. That called the "step."

Your airspeed is also slightly higher making the trip faster. My reasons were two-fold: to keep from having to refuel again and to scare the crap out of Eddie.

As I passed through about 9,000 ft. the old girl went off the first time with her arm involuntarily lifting a few inches. Eddie saw that and screamed "She's alive!!" I pretended not to hear. "SHE'S MOVING!" he yelled.

I looked back and Eddie was now in an upright fetal position with both legs drawn to his chest with his arms folded over them. I could hold it no longer. I was nearly bent over in peals of laughter, which only pissed Eddie off because he knew I had gotten him.

"You ain't seen nothing' yet..." I said between high pitched giggles.

Just then she farted, loudly. Eddie screamed like a little girl. I turned as far as I could in my seat and reached back and put my hand on his arm. "Eddie! Take a breath and relax. You're gonna faint." He unfolded some. "She's quite dead, I assure you. I'm messing with your head."

"Sum-bitch!" he retorted.

"Bodies do that. Enjoy the ride." I laughed.

"So there were never any girls in the first place?" he yelled. I said, "Nope." and started to laugh again. "Shut the hell up!" hollered Eddie. I had reached about 13,000 feet, leveled off, and set the trim in a slight dive.

I had forgotten I was still climbing because I was laughing so hard. Anything over 10,000 feet for 30 minutes and you'll need supplemental oxygen or weird things like passing out start to happen. I was getting light-headed.

Well, I wasn't done with Eddie yet. The flight was fairly uneventful until we got to within 80 miles or so from Hammond where I would refuel, drop off Eddie, and proceed on to New Orleans. My radio had gone out and the weather had become so fierce that I was flat-hatting low on the deck circling water towers so I could read the city names painted on them to determine where I was.

Eddie was in a state of panic by now. I was taking it seriously, apologizing and trying to reassure him everything was going to be okay. But every time I buzzed a water tower, he would return to his fetal position saying things like "There's already one God damned dead person here and I don't want to join her!!"

I made the decision to land at McComb, Mississippi, north of Hammond, and wait out the weather. As I lined up for final at McComb, Eddy thought we were crashing and started praying which sent me into fits of high pitched laughter.

But we did land.

Once on the ground, Eddie popped the door open, jumped over the body and hopped out. I was busy shutting things down and when I looked up, Eddie was stomping off the airport. I hollered, "Eddie! Where are you going?!" "HOME!" he yelled over his shoulder. I watched as he hailed a taxi. I would later learn he went to the bus station and hopped on a Greyhound back to Louisiana. I later reimbursed him for the ticket.

It took Eddie three months to really forgive me. For me, it was three agonizing months of watching over my back for the inevitable payback, which never came. That was Eddie's way of paying me back. Three months of suspense and paranoia.

When I finally caught up with Eddie years later, I had called his office and his secretary asked my name. I told her. She exclaimed, "Oh! You're the guy that took him flying to get the dead body." It was 30 years later and he was still telling the story.

Chapter Seven

Vicious Little Sh*t

Prissy was a rail thin, delicate woman. What attracted her to Ocelots, I can't say. She was rather artsy in nature and perhaps it was because Salvador Dalí owned one named Babou. But I can say that for a time life was made either interesting or terrifying because of that cat.

As I previously said, the first time I met Prissy was in a bar at a bowling alley. She was standing there holding the ocelot beast while wearing welding gloves which had leather gauntlets that nearly reached her elbows.

She needed them. Ocelots have razor sharp claws and their way of keeping an edge on them is by slicing open the small animals and rodents they hunt in the jungle. If small animals or rodents aren't available, humans will do.

Now, for some time, I lived in the hanger where I was perfectly happy sleeping on a cot next to an old airplane, nestled among parachute packs hanging on racks made of galvanized pipe.

But, after a short time, maybe weeks, I was given a small room with a fold-out couch in the adjacent portable building. That was even better, as I could set up a television (which only received two channels) and store some snack foods. I had moved up in the world. The only problem was I had no bathroom.

There were two public restrooms outside adjacent to the building where I could relieve myself and shave using cold water. Cold water presented no problems for me as I had done that numerous mornings in the military.

But, in order to bathe, I would have to go over to Leon and Prissy's small, one-bedroom caretaker's house just behind my quarters. There, I would have access to a full bathroom and bath tub, which I did once every few days. Life was good -- except for Crossbow the ocelot.

Now, allow me to refresh your memory regarding ocelots. The ocelot is similar in appearance to a domestic cat. Its fur resembles that of a clouded leopard or jaguar and was once regarded as particularly valuable. As a result, hundreds of thousands of ocelots were killed for their fur. They are also known as "dwarf leopards." But mostly, they are "vicious little shits," as a friend recently remarked.

The bathroom had a claw foot bathtub and sat about five inches off the floor. The space under the tub was Crossbow's favorite hiding place. I did not discover this until my encounter with her while taking a bath.

Typically, I would walk over to the house after Leon and Prissy had finished their bathroom business in the morning. I would shave in luxuriously warm water and set about taking my bath.

Crossbow would silently lie in waiting under the tub. She didn't purr, move or otherwise make a sound. I would strip, run some water and get in to stretch out and enjoy the warmth. Soon, I would rinse away the shampoo and step out to retrieve my towel.

As I did, Crossbow would strike out with a lightening swipe of her paw across my ankle just above the joint. The resulting laceration, which should have gotten stitches, but never did, would leave me standing in a pool of blood and screaming bloody murder. Crossbow then retreated as far back under the tub as she could, out of reach, to gloat over her successful attack.

She did this to me several times. I got smart thereafter poking around under the tub with a broom handle to make sure she wasn't there.

Now these attacks not only took place in the bathroom but could happen anywhere in the house.

Ordinarily, Leon, Prissy and I had the majority of our evening meals at home. Prissy would head over to the house just before quitting time and fix us all some supper.

In addition to the threat of ocelot attack, I also had to gird myself for Leon's dinner table attacks. I'm told many Cajuns eat this way, but I cannot prove it. When Prissy called, Leon and I would race to wash our hands. I say "race" because eating with Leon was a competition to avoid starvation. Once he got to the table, he would reach out and take the first dish that caught his eye, and turn it nearly upside down and shovel out the majority of its contents.

Then, with the next food item, he would perform the same act until he had heaping piles of rice or red beans or chicken or whatever it was we were having that night on his plate. He usually left just enough for Prissy and I to eat so we could fend off malnutrition.

So the contest became one of getting enough to eat. He wasn't being rude. He was just being Leon.

My cultivated survival technique was to sacrifice whatever he reached for first and reach for something else while he was shoveling his on his plate, get some for myself and then hand the dish to Prissy.

That way, we got enough of at least several items before he could strike again. The really infuriating part was that Leon would eat all of each item on his plate completely before moving on to the next. It made for interesting meal times.

Well, the result of this preoccupation was that I wasn't on guard for Crossbow. She might have been on the refrigerator top just behind my chair or merely sauntering through the house looking for targets. Many times, her lair was on top of the refrigerator, nestled among the loaves of bread and Saltine and Ritz cracker boxes. I have to say, however, she was polite and refrained from engaging her targets until we finished eating.

The danger, for me, was finishing my meal and pushing back in my chair. That somehow or another triggered in her the need to engage in a leaping, snarling, jump with her claws un-holstered while looking for my jugular as she landed on my shoulders.

In short order, I had learned to push back from the table, suddenly diving sideways as she went airborne from the refrigerator. Missing, she would hit the ground hissing and I would grab the broom and fight my way out the back door. Prissy would just laugh a high pitched squeal thinking the nightly after-dinner show was hilarious. I put up with it for months and was always relieved when someone suggested we go out for supper.

One day, I went over to the house to retrieve some drinks from the refrigerator. I cautiously approached the refrigerator door while keeping one eye out for the beast. I didn't see it. Still looking about and anticipating an attack, I quickly opened the door, snatched two sodas out and closed the door, stepping back quickly thinking I might have missed something vis-à-vis the devil cat.

I was continuing to sweep the room with my eyes when I happened to notice the tip of Crossbow's tale behind the refrigerator. It was not moving or twitching as it usually did. I set the drinks down on the table and retrieved the broom from across the kitchen and returned.

Cautiously, nervously, I poked the tip of the tail with the broom handle and rapidly took a defensive position in the event Crossbow exploded into action. Nothing. The tail didn't move.

I prodded it again. No response. I thrust at it once more. Nada. I then set the broom aside and pulled the refrigerator out a few inches and snatched a fast look behind it like a cop entering a room. Crossbow was still. No movement. I could see she wasn't breathing. She was dead! I did a little silent jig right then and there – a victory dance. Ding Dong! The witch was dead!

Then it hit me! Prissy! She's going to go nuts when she discovers this. What am I going to do? She'll think I did it. She knew I hated that animal along with most of our jumpers who had encounters with it.

While I was worrying about that, I pulled the refrigerator a back little further and drug the cat out by its tail. It had a piece of asbestos insulation hanging from its mouth!

That damn cat had been eating the insulation out of the back wall of the refrigerator. No wonder it was dead -- may as well have been eating glass. Still...what was I going do? So, I made up a story that went something like this:

I went to get the drinks. I opened the back door. The cat shot between my legs and into the field beyond.

Yeah, that'll work. So, I went back to the office with the drinks and told the story.

Before doing that I quickly found a box and put the cat in it. I then snuck it over to my room and locked it inside. Once I told the story, Leon and I conducted a fake search. Finding nothing as I knew we would, we both assured Prissy it would come back on its own when it got hungry.

The next day, I made up an excuse that I had to go to town for something, and squirreled the box into the car. I took it a taxidermist friend of mine and paid him to mount and stuff it. He said it would be ready in a few weeks. I turned to leave his shop and sarcastically quipped in jest, "While you're at it, put wheels on it and a ring in its nose and she can pull the damn thing around behind her."

It was an innocent piece of sarcasm and I thought nothing of it until I went back a few weeks later to pick it up. There stood a dead, stuffed Crossbow with beady glass eyes mounted atop four roller skate wheels with a brass ring adorning its nose. Oh crap!

So, I paid the guy what I owed him for what I thought was going to be a comfort to Prissy. Now, look what I got. So, back to the airport I went.

Now, I've always been a little bit of a smooth talker. When I got back to the airport, I made a big deal of how I had found the cat, dead, and I wasn't trying to be a smartass or funny and how I made the silly remark, and how what I'd done was really supposed to be a comfort to Prissy.

She bought it – hesitantly, suspiciously – but she bought it. Leon knew well enough to stand back, stifle any laughter or remarks he might have, and not get killed. But the whole time I was spreading it on with Prissy, he was standing behind her rolling his eyes at me while wearing his trademark Cheshire grin.

Time passed.

Now, Leon and I hoped that was the end of living with a terror. But it wasn't to be. Leon was increasingly bothered by Prissy's pining over the loss of her beloved Crossbow. She had buried my tribute. She couldn't bear to look at it.

So, Leon started looking in the newspapers to see if he might find a replacement beast. He did. The Times-Picayune newspaper in New Orleans carried an ad from man wanting to give away a male ocelot. Males are usually somewhat bigger than the females and were reported to be more docile. We made arrangements with the gentleman to meet us at Lakefront Airport in New Orleans one evening. So, we fired up the little four-place Cessna 170 and took off telling Prissy that we were going to get some aircraft parts.

Once there, it had become completely dark, but we met the man and took the cat. He had put it into a cardboard box and tied it up with string. We looked at each other and figured the box would be secure enough to fly home with. We didn't want the thing loose in the airplane, at night, over the 27 mile expanse of Lake Pontchatrain. We set the box on the rear seat, did a preflight walk around -- a check of the exterior of the airplane -- and then got permission from the control tower to take off.

Once over the water, on a direct flight path back to Hammond, I turned to look at the box. The only light I had was a very small, very dim, overhead light that I had switched on. The box was open and laying on its side. "Leon! The cat's out!" I yelled over the engine noise.

So, while he flew, I started checking under our seats. Nothing. At least, if this one was docile, we might get back home without bleeding from the ankles or some other body part.

I began feeling around underneath the instrument panel with my hand and wasn't happy about the prospect of maybe pulling back a nub, but we had to find that cat. Not finding anything under the panel, I crawled over the seats into the back, which was occupied by the one long bench seat running across the cabin and tried to see under it.

We had no flashlight, so I wound up feeling around under the seat. Nothing again. Leon hollered, "You think that thing got all the way back in the tail section?" I said, "Maybe somehow it got out of the box on the ground before we took off?" "Maybe." he said, but he didn't believe it. I didn't either. It had to be in the rear of the aircraft.

The fuselage behind the back seat was an empty cavern, a tunnel made of aluminum that contained only some electrical wiring and stainless steel cables running the length of the plane that operate the rear flight surfaces. If the cat was back there, it was going to have to stay there until we landed.

Leon said he was having no difficulty flying, the cables seemed free, and we continued on. Soon, the long dotted string of white runway lights appeared in the distance and we landed and hurriedly taxied onto the airport apron, the parking area, and parked.

I jumped out and found a flashlight. Shining it into the compartment, we could see nothing but the wires and cables. We talked about it. Maybe it had somehow gotten out on the ground at Lakefront? We agreed we understood how it could have done that; that perhaps, it had done so as we were outside doing the pre-flight walk-around and we just didn't see it get out. That had to have been it. We tied the airplane down and went to bed.

The next morning...

I got out of bed, walked out of my room and into the humid morning air, then went to the public latrine and relieved myself. Soon, Leon would come out of the small caretaker's house, stumbling alongside me, yawning, holding a cup of instant coffee and join me to stretch and scratch his rear-end.

Most mornings, we stood there looking out across the expanse of the airport, watching low hanging clouds of fog moving across the horizon and starting to fade away in the warmth of the rising sun. We said little, mostly innocent small talk. We were about 30 feet away from the 170 with its white wings glistening with morning dew.

After a few minutes, we turned to go open the office, grab the truck keys and wait until Prissy joined us so we go get breakfast at the M&L Dairy Bar where we had a credit account. That was our usual morning routine. They let us eat on the cuff and we paid the bill at the end of the month.

Just as we started for the office, he and I heard a growl and hissing. We looked at each other in astonishment. The noise was coming from the 170. We slowly turned and approached the airplane as the growling persisted accompanied by muffled thumping.

We slowly crept up to the rear of the airplane and listened intently as the sound continued. As we got within about three feet of the airplane's tail section, it struck both of us simultaneously that the creature had gotten wedged in the very confined last bit of tail section and was struggling to get out. We simply missed it the night before.

I ran to get some tools and Leon ran to get the welding gloves and a flashlight.

He made the decision to crawl into the fuselage to retrieve the cat. It would be very hot soon and the heat would kill it quickly. After an hour's struggle, he handed the cat out to me. I laid it on the ground. It was barely breathing. Leon got out of the airplane and picked up the limp mini-leopard just as Prissy walked up to see what happened. The cat's eyes were crazed and it was as flaccid as cooked spaghetti.

Prissy gasped and said, "What the hell is that?" Leon said, "It's Crossbow's replacement. We picked it up in New Orleans last night." Prissy reached out to take the nearly dead cat and held it in her arms. "It'll be alright," Leon said, "it just needs some food and rest." Prissy kissed Leon on the cheek and took the cat to the house. He and I, proud of ourselves, jumped in our little green Econoline truck and headed for breakfast.

In the end, it turned out, the cat, which was never named, hated Prissy and wasn't docile at all, at least to her. After a few weeks, she demanded we take it back, which we did – to the New Orleans zoo. In the middle of the night, we made a deposit over the zoo's fence and flew back home.

The era of ocelots at Southern Parachute Center was finally over. Nobody had to watch where they were walking and we could take baths safely or finish a meal without acrobatics once again. Leon, however, was still a supper time threat.

Chapter Eight

Demos and Maniacs

There was only one activity I enjoyed more than jumping at the airport. That was making demonstration jumps at various functions and events. The places we made those jumps varied widely and covered everything from the opening of new shopping centers to county fairs to car dealerships and racetracks.

The atmosphere was always festive, we usually got fed and pretty girls were everywhere. It was what you might call a "target rich" environment when it came to picking up women. And we always had a leg up on the local guys who didn't jump. Our bravery and machismo shone brightly.

One day, we got a call from a local Chevrolet dealer who was having a special sale and wanted us to make three jumps in one day into his dealership parking lot. Now, we didn't actually get the call ourselves. One of our occasional jumpers, Major Goodman, did. He arranged it himself and needed the use of our airplane, a pilot and few other jumpers. I elected to make the jumps with him and Leon flew. One other jumper, Herb, from Baton Rouge, made up the third jumper.

A little about Major Goodman or "Goody" as we called him:

Goody had a reputation for being bat-shit crazy and he was -- literally. As one example, we had scheduled night jumps for a number of jumpers who needed them to satisfy their parachutist license requirements. Night jumps and water jumps along with a certain number of jumps from various altitudes had to be made and witnessed in order to qualify for different license ratings.

I was selected to ensure that each jumper had the proper equipment, was briefed about what to expect, and to also make sure they had the right kind of light attached to their helmet. There would be more than one jumper in the air at a time, and the light was needed to avoid collisions.

Goody showed up to jump and my heart sank the minute I saw his car turn into the parking lot. No matter what anyone else was thinking, Leon and I knew then the gloves were off of what was, so far, a well-planned, safe event.

We could have said "no" to him and that would have been it. But we didn't, we just watched him like hawks.

So, the sun set and it got dark enough to proceed. I checked out and briefed the first three jumpers. They got into the airplane and Leon took off with them.

Night jumps present some extreme hazards.

First of all, it's dark. Free fall at night is tough because there is no horizon reference. Second, once you open your parachute, you can't see that it opened properly. If, after opening, you feel your rate of descent is too fast, you have probably experienced a main canopy malfunction, so you must deploy your reserve parachute. In those days, unlike today, reserve parachutes had to be hand-thrown to deploy them and that could be tricky even in the daylight.

The last big hazard is landing. Even under a good, well-functioning parachute, landings were awkward because you couldn't see the ground coming at you. So you could easily not be ready for it and get your wind knocked out.

Having a freshly packed reserve parachute was mandatory. And I made sure to check everyone's reserve along with the rest of their gear very closely.

Back then, a small reserve parachute was worn on the lower chest attached to the main parachute harness and was very tightly packed, given the immense amount of material that had to be packed into a very limited space.

Goody shuffles up to me. I swept my flashlight across him and noticed that his reserve appeared mushy, not full and tight. I asked him when it was last packed as I groped the pack. It felt like it was full of paper, not nylon.

"What do you have in there?" I inquire. He looks at me as if I will be approving of the answer. "A fifth of whiskey wrapped in newspaper in case I land off the airport and I have to camp out." was his response, almost as if he was proud of his ingenuity and survival skills. I benched him then and there. No night jump for Goody on my watch.

Supposedly Goody had a degree in chemistry and was a pyrotechnics expert. He did sell us some chemicals once to add to the cooling system of our little truck which proceeded to eat up all the cooling hoses. Not surprising.

A rumor circulated that there was a stray cat that slept on his porch swing, and he hated the cat. So he mixed up a batch of nitroglycerin on his kitchen stove and was going to use some of it to blow the cat to kingdom come the next time it jumped up on his swing. He blew the entire front of his house off instead.

Another tale spread about how he donned scuba gear and dove into the lake on the University of Southern Mississippi's campus at Hattiesburg and hunted ducks from underwater with a spear gun.

Then there was the time he landed at our airport in his little two seat airplane, a Globe Swift. He wanted to make a spectacular arrival and affixed a military smoke bomb, which is an incendiary device, to the tail of his airplane. As he approached for landing, he activated the smoke bomb with a long piece of cord he had strung from the tail to the cockpit. When he taxied up, the tail of the aircraft was aflame and it took two fire extinguishers to put it out.

The icing on the cake was the time he landed his airplane on a street in downtown Baton Rouge and taxied to his apartment and parked. He lost his pilot's license over that one.

Now back to the demo at the Chevrolet dealer. I made it harshly and perfectly clear to Goody that I would be the jumpmaster and in charge of the jumps. He would sit where I said to in the airplane, get out at the spot I told him to, and he would stay the hell away from me.

We loaded up for the first jump. I was familiar with the Chevrolet place as was Leon and we proceeded to about 7,200 feet and circled over the dealership. We waited on a signal from the ground as to when to jump. The signal was supposed to be white smoke from a military-type smoke grenade.

When the smoke appeared on the ground, I got Leon lined up on jump run. The order of exit would be me first, Goody second and Herb last. I gave Leon the minor corrections he needed and when the time was right, I was gone. I free fell to about 2,500 feet and opened.

After opening, the very first order of business was to see where Goody was. He was well above me about 500 feet. No problem, no danger from him. I began steering towards the parking lot. In a few seconds, I began to notice small, white trails of smoke flying downwards past me towards the ground. Then I looked up and noticed several small holes near the top on my canopy.

Goody had opened his parachute, somehow lit a cigar, and was now throwing small fireworks-type smoke bombs towards the ground. He was lighting them with the cigar. He rained at least 50 of them down during his descent -- several of them penetrating my canopy on their way to the ground. He was too far away to hear my screams to get him to stop.

As I got to within about 150 feet of the ground, I started to see people running in all directions as billows of white smoke wafted through the dealership parking lot. There was so much smoke it was difficult to even see the ground clearly. Soon, I realized the smoke wasn't smoke at all.

It was clouds of toxic vapor created by a mosquito fogging machine that Goody had given to his wife and instructed her to fire it up when she saw the airplane coming. She was asphyxiating everyone on the ground and now us. My eyes began to tear up and even though I landed alright, I had to grope my way around to even see where I was walking. Leon had sent someone from the airport to pick us up and drive us the 30 miles or so back to the airport. Herb and I bundled into the car and left Goody there to explain. But it wasn't the end for Goody.

We got back to airport and aired out ourselves and our equipment. In an hour or so, Goody followed. He pleaded for us to go with him again as he had committed and been paid to make several more jumps for the dealer that day. We simply shook our heads "no," and hoped he'd disappear. He didn't.

He cornered Herb who had his own airplane there that day and he talked Herb into, at least, flying him. Herb liked the thought of being paid and a deal was struck. The last I heard of this and, for that matter, Goody, was that Herb got him over the dealership.

When Goody stepped out and put his foot on the landing gear to make an exit, he slipped. His boot got entangled with a hydraulic brake line, a small piece of copper tubing, and he fell off only to remain attached to the landing gear hanging upside down dangling by one leg screaming.

He started yelling at Herb that he was going pull his parachute and that would snatch him away. That scared Herb to death thinking that the parachute might billow out over the plane's tail, get entangled, and they would crash and die. Herb began to weave and roll the airplane violently from side to side and eventually he shook Goody free.

I have wondered many times what asylum he was locked up in. And, I've feared for the other inmates.

Chapter Nine

Esmeralda

For a time, we owned Esmeralda, the mannequin. She was a life size rubber dummy with a big chest and all the right features. You can only suppose what her real purpose was.

We would keep her, most days, in the little lobby of our office at the airport, standing upright, modeling all the latest, coolest parachute gear that we sold. She had everything -- a new yellow jumpsuit, a shiny new helmet, black jump boots, the best parachute, goggles – everything. She stood in her corner silently every day, bothering no one, but being eyed now-and-then by the occasional horny jumper who had been a long time without some love.

Once and a while, she would get to see the outside world when we set up a display somewhere to attract new first jump students. That could be at a shopping center or at the local college where we would set up a card table and a few folding chairs, pass out brochures and chat up the passers-by. Then she would return to her respective corner to await yet one more trip to the outside world.

Now jumpers are a lot that are easily bored. Let's say the cloud cover is too low to jump safely and that you have a gang of five or six of jumpers sitting around the airport telling war stories and twiddling their thumbs.

Somebody is going to come up with something that makes no sense and is probably dangerous, to pass the time. That's how Esmeralda got into trouble. And, I have to say, that I'm surprised it didn't happen sooner.

One day that was the precise situation: low clouds, easily high enough to fly but too low to jump. Leon birthed this idea, and because it was Leon who everyone looked up to, that gave it immediate credibility. Even though, had Leon thought it through longer he would have realized it wasn't going to do his local image any good, but he did not and pressed ahead.

I could tell by looking at Prissy when Leon spoke of it, that she did not approve, but she also thought it was going to be too funny to pass up, so she kept quiet. In a moment of stillness, we were sitting around staring at the floor and Leon looked up at Esmeralda and said, "Let's drop her over Hammond with no parachute. Nude."

I was immediately on-board as the idea fit my style precisely. "Yeah!" I said, not thinking even remotely of any consequences.

Somebody jumped up and grabbed Esmeralda and drug her into the hanger and threw her up on the packing table and started disrobing her. Perhaps in lust, I don't know. Soon, he drug her back into the lobby, and deposited her unceremoniously in a heap on the lobby floor, grinning.

Leon said, "Who's going with me?" while looking dead at me. He knew I was in. We picked her up and headed for the 170. Leon jumped in the pilot's seat and started flipping switches. I ran back to the hanger and grabbed an emergency parachute and quickly put it on and ran back to the airplane which was sitting at an idle waiting on me. I put Esmeralda into the seat next to me and Leon started to taxi out for take-off.

We rolled down runway 36 and lifted off, banked and turned towards Hammond. The distance to town was so short we would be over the main intersection in the tiny town in five minutes. Once over the center of town, Leon made about 5 circuits circling overhead at about 1000 feet to get everybody's attention on the ground.

The circling also gave everybody from the parachute center time enough to get there to watch the fun.

Then he rolled in on what I knew to be a jump (drop) run. I kept my eyes on him. He would give me a signal to drop. Shortly, he raised his right hand and gave me a thumbs-up. I had her perched in the open door and literally kicked her out. She fell away. He rolled in a sharp banking turn so we had a clear view of her impact.

Esmeralda only weighed about 50 pounds and she fell lazily. I could see a number of townsfolk on the sidewalks going about their business but looking up at our airplane. In a few seconds she sailed right into the middle of the town's busiest intersection and landed with a slight bounce smack dab in the middle of the street. I saw one woman collapse and sit down right on the sidewalk right where she stood. But, for the most part, everyone else froze in their tracks, not believing their eyes.

By that time, Leon and I were literally rolling around the cabin nearly in tears. He was still at the controls but he was bent over in laughter. I was lying across the backseat holding my sides. To us, it was a totally innocent hilarious act.

We'd land, jump in the truck and head to town to retrieve Esmeralda. Everyone would have a good laugh and we had shaken off the boredom. Turns out, we didn't need to drive to town. Town came to us.

As we turned on final to land, I was looking out the window towards town and saw, in the distance, a red flashing light on a car on the highway coming at a high rate of speed towards the airport as we crossed over the road and landed. By the time we rolled into airport parking area, a black and white cop car was turning onto the terminal road. I thought, *"Here we go."*

As we exited the airplane, I could see the cop car sitting in the parking lot with Esmeralda's feet sticking out the back window. Leon looked at me and gave me a *"We've had it."* shrug. He went through the office door first, me trailing close behind.

Inside, everybody including the cop who had brought her back was in peals of laughter. The young cop was one of just a few that Hammond had on what it called a police force at the time. We knew him well.

He proceeded to give Leon a fierce mock chewing out using phrases like "civic responsibility" and "respect for others" between giggles.

Leon stood with head hung, his hands crossed in front of him as if he was taking it seriously and was in a state of remorse.

"Leon," the cop finally said, "I have to do what I'm about to do. I don't want to, but I have to tell the Chief and the Mayor something that will appease them." He proceeded to pull a ticket book out of his back pocket and wrote Leon a ticket for littering and handed it to him grinning, saying, "Now, get that damn dummy out of my car."

The fine was $25. Not bad for the laughs.

Chapter Ten

A World of Our Own

The one major thing that always fascinated me about my time at Southern Parachute Center is how focused we were on what we were doing and how little anything else mattered.

During the time, the fight for racial equality was at a fever pitch, the "war" in Viet Nam was ramping up fiercely, Martin Luther King and Bobby Kennedy were assassinated. Hippies were busy creating the perfect world. The draft was sucking up an entire generation of young guys, and turning them into soldiers. Many of them would not return and many of those who did would wind up junkies. The world was changing and heaving to and fro, and those of us who jumped at the parachute center cared little for anything else but the next jump, the next beer, the next jump and on it went.

It's not that we weren't aware. It's that it didn't matter, and we had other things to do, and we weren't apologetic about it. We were having fun. We did know of these things. Many of our jumpers who came and went were being affected, mainly by military service.

Now and then, we would get word of one of our own killed-in-action, and for a day, that would make us quiet – reflective. But, the end result was always sitting around having a few beers and telling exaggerated tales of the dearly departed's crazy deeds and laughing wildly about the outcomes. It was our way of grieving.

Life in Louisiana was sometimes problematic -- particularly where it concerned race. Most of us didn't note much whether our jumpers were white, black or anything else. They were jumpers. It didn't matter to us. We didn't concern ourselves with it. But, the world close by was highly concerned.

It was the Deep South. In the surrounding counties resided the highest concentration of the Ku Klux Klan in the country at the time. We never spoke of it. I guess our policy was you don't bother us, we don't bother you. There was only one time I nearly stepped over the line.

The local media had written and spoken for weeks about a planned freedom march from Bogalusa, Louisiana, to Baton Rouge in August of 1967. We knew it was coming. We also knew that the route of the march would take it just outside the airport on Highway 190.

At the intersection of the airport road and Highway 190 was a "rest area," more of a picnic and parking area where travelers could pull in and take a break. In the past, many of our jumpers had parked their campers there to overnight.

I was my usual unconscious self, more content to teach students, make jumps, and scout the next female conquest. Most of us never spoke of the impending march. It just wasn't important to us at all. The local radio station, which we listened to during the day, was posting periodic updates about the march's progress. We knew the march was within about two miles of the airport.

The state police had made it clear to everyone to stay away from the roads and bridges along the march's route. They also sent out explosives teams to ensure the bridges along the route had not been set with dynamite. They had horse-mounted troopers and troopers on foot accompanying the marchers en route to Baton Rouge.

The jump activity for the day had pretty much settled into a lull and we were all sitting around the lounge eating sandwiches and drinking soda pop. One particularly memorable character had shown up for the day – Rick.

Rick wore full braces on both legs and could walk pretty well on his own. He had gotten both legs caught up in his suspension lines while his parachute was opening over Lucedale, Mississippi, one day.

When the canopy exploded open, the opening snatched both of his legs out of their sockets and crippled him. But Rick stayed involved in the jump community by showing up at our drop zone and other drop zones around the South to party and have fun. He always had the sexiest of women on his arm and drove a Jaguar convertible.

Leon and I were sitting next to each other on the couch in the lounge laughing and joking with everybody when Leon says, "You know what I think we oughta do?" The room fell silent. He paused dramatically. In a few seconds, to the hushed room, he said, "I think we oughta make a demo jump into the rest area when the marchers come."

"Yeah!" I said. I always said "Yeah!" I continued, "Let's do that."

We had been listening to the live reports on the radio and knew the marchers were going to stop at the rest area and take a break and make speeches.

Leon jumped up and said, "I'm going to gas up the 170. You -- *pointing at me* -- go get a rig and meet me when I get back." This meant I was going to make the jump into the rest area. I didn't give a thought to the possible consequences. He taxied over to the gas pump. I grabbed my gear and got it on. I was waiting on the ramp when he returned and I piled in.

A quick take-off and we turned towards the rest area. All I could think about was hitting that little rest area which was very, very small. And, it was surrounded by trees and power lines. I had completely forgotten about state policemen on horseback guarding the marchers who were also accompanied by armed national guard troops.

I didn't give any thought to the fact that those guys might get it in their heads that I was a crazed Klansman with 20 pounds of TNT strapped to my chest carrying a detonator in my hand ready to rain death down on the crowd.

As we came across on the first pass to throw a wind streamer, I was thinking only about hitting my landing spot.

Nothing else.

Once over the rest area, I threw the rolled up wind streamer out. Wind streamers are foot-wide strips of yellow crepe paper usually about 15 feet long used to track the direction of the wind over your target. Once unfurled, the weighted end starts its descent towards the ground and drifts along with the prevailing breeze.

Wherever it lands, you fly upwind an equal distance, opposite of that spot, and that is where you exit. Then you steer the parachute to make small adjustments in course and, hopefully, land where you need to. We circled and watched as the wind streamer descended. It landed about 50 yards from the rest area back on the airport.

We circled back and started a jump run. I gave Leon the small course corrections he needed and once over my spot, I exited, free fell a bit then hooked my rip cord with my right hand and pulled it. Whumpf! My canopy opened and I settled in to make the descent into the rest area.

I also had given no thought to the fact that I was jumping a homemade parachute we had dubbed "The Skyhook." The Hook was huge, nearly 25 percent bigger than other parachutes and had been dyed garish pink and baby crap green.

It was made from a patchwork of salvaged parachutes by Leon some time before that, and then passed on to me. It wasn't my favorite canopy to jump because its turns were sluggish. It had been modeled after the latest and greatest new parachute to hit the market, the Para Commander. The PC was the fast moving, fast turning Corvette of its day. The Hook was a poor substitute.

But there I was trying to hit a drop zone that measured approximately 50 feet by 50 feet full of possibly hostile people with guns. I still wasn't really thinking them. Yet.

As I was descending into the rest area, I started to notice the mounted police moving up through the crowd in the rest area. At about 500 feet, I was seriously considering turning off and landing outside the rest area on the airport proper -- but didn't. I had my pride, you know?

I continued the descent into the rest area. At about 200 feet, close enough to make out detail, I started see the state police drawing guns and pointing them in my direction. The crowd on the ground had moved to the edges of the park forming a big empty circle in the middle. Several of the state police were armed with rifles.

I started to sense then that I could be in big trouble. But nobody fired, and I landed perfectly in the center of that empty space. And, I landed upright without falling down, a stand-up landing. For the briefest second, I thought I heard somebody clap. I was wrong. Someone had racked a bullet into the chamber of a gun.

I didn't budge. I just stood there for a second making sure everyone could see I had empty hands, and then I said in a very loud voice, "Ya'll having a party?"

There was no response – nothing but abject silence from the uneasy glowering, tense crowd. About that time, Rick came screaming down the road in the Jaguar with his beauty of the day sitting beside him. At the entrance to the rest area, he slid to a stop in a spray of gravel.

Then he slowly pulled into the rest area and came to a stop next to me with a big smile on his face and said, innocently, loudly, "This is last time I'm gonna pick you up when you miss the airport." I laughed nervously. I then picked up my canopy and bundled it in my arms and fell into the little space behind Rick's seat in the Jag. He wheeled backwards and turned around and we headed back to the office laughing hysterically.

We got back and everybody was slapping me on the back. Leon was laughing and Prissy was rolling her eyes. I was the hero of the day. Out on the road, the march continued on to Baton Rouge. The whole affair was forgotten about until...

About three o'clock in the morning I woke up startled and sat completely upright in bed. The full realization of what could have happened was playing itself out in my head ending with me dead, slumped in my harness, as I landed. I shivered just a little. In the future, I would be a bit more questioning of Leon's great ideas.

There would be many more of Leon's great ideas to come. But, at least, I can claim a very small piece of the history in the fight for civil rights.

Chapter Eleven

Gross Diversions

There were periods of slump at the Center. With winter's cold and the low clouds and the rains of early spring, there were lean times – times of boredom and restlessness. Prissy usually sought a job as a church secretary and left Leon and I to our own devices.

Occasionally, we had an extra jumper hang out for a few weeks, perhaps having come from far away to jump with us. But during those times, they would get in very little jumping. Mostly, it was just Leon and I on the prowl looking for something to do once the cleaning and aircraft maintenance had been seen to.

One day, word got to us that the Green Door was holding a red beans and rice eating competition. It wasn't for me, as I would maybe get two plates full down. But this game was right up Leon's alley and he was all up for it, not eating a thing since breakfast to prepare. Later that day, we jumped in the little Econoline truck and headed for town.

The Green Door was a college bar and a popular hangout for the students of Southeastern Louisiana University.

The place was dark and reeked of urine, but the beer was cold and free flowing. Usually the juke box never got quiet. It seemed Wilson Pickett was always rocking out. There was always a string of regulars sitting at the bar.

When we arrived, a small group was already setting up a table to eat from in the back room and the smell of red beans and rice was heavy in the air, wafting forth from the small kitchen in the back. Leon refused a beer to keep his stomach empty, but I grabbed a Jax. Jax is a New Orleans brewed beer that tastes something akin to what dishwater must taste like, but it was cheap and I was perpetually broke.

A little about the dish red beans and rice. It is a Louisiana staple, much like gumbo or jambalaya -- the latter two being more a soup or stew. Red beans and rice is a thick, spicy sauce heavy with red beans, a substantial legume. It is often served as a side dish, but more often than not, in poorer households, as a main course. It is substantial stick-to-your-ribs food. Cheap, easy to make and versatile, it may also contain chicken, beef or seafood in the recipe.

The bartender called the contest to order and Leon was chosen along with three young college kids to compete first. The competition went something like this:

The food was free. You could order one plate at a time -- a standard dinner plate -- filled with red beans and rice. You could ask for as many plates as you could eat clean. There was a five-minute-per-plate rule. If you weren't completely done with each plate you ordered within five minutes, you had to leave the table and a fresh face took your seat. If you had to leave and throw up, you were disqualified.

That also meant that if you threw up in place, you could keep eating, but you had to clean it up later. Most everyone who needed to puke ran to the john.

The contestants took their seats. I could tell by the smart-ass remarks coming from everyone at the table, that the cocky kids thought they would out eat Leon quickly and send him packing. Leon just sat there silently flashing the Cheshire grin. Here's what they didn't know. Leon was all stomach from the base of his Adam's apple down to his knees.

Countless times, I had seen him walk into a restaurant and order gumbo by the pot full. The waitress would arrive, take his order, which was going to be gumbo served over rice, and before she left the table, he would stop her and ask her to bring his in a pot, not a bowl.

The waitresses who knew him didn't question it. They didn't blink an eye when he asked. He would be the only one at the table eating from a pot or a large tureen. I often thought that Prissy would ultimately die of embarrassment. But she didn't.

Many a time, we gathered at his mother's grand old southern home at Ponchatoula. She had a big swimming pool and large overhanging oaks and the jumpers were always welcome for food, beer and night of dancing to Zydeco music. There were always two or three bushels of boiled blue crab ready to eat along with the obligatory hot dogs and hamburgers.

The crab is what Leon and I always zeroed in on. Many of the other guests didn't eat much crab because they really didn't know how. It's an art form involving a lot of shell-cracking and meat-picking. A lot of folks also just don't have the patience for it.

It wasn't uncommon for the two of us to sit under the trees and eat two or more bushels of crab on our own, all while washing it down with a case of beer between us. We'd start eating at sundown and when daylight started to set in, we'd just be finishing.

Back at the Green Door, the first plate orders were delivered and forks started to fly. Leon easily went through his first three plates. One of the kids started to turn green after his second plate and the other two got through their third plate, but one of them balked at ordering a forth.

The green-faced kid ran for the head. His replacement took a seat and a plate was set in front of him. The one that balked went ahead and ordered, but only got the first few bites down before heading for the door. Leon finished his forth plate and grinned again. He was just getting started.

Now, the last rule of the game was this: If you didn't out-eat the leader in terms of the total number of plates finished, you could not win. So, after the fifth plate, no one could possibly catch up.

People took their seats against Leon just to see how many plates he could eat. So, person after person belly-upped and ordered a plate, most only lasting one plate before leaving the table. At Leon's fourteenth plate, the Green Door ran out of red beans and rice and the contest was over. Nobody could out-eat the man. I helped him out to the truck where he promptly threw up on the sidewalk.

Now, another way we liked to kill boredom was going fishing.

Leon had been a Louisiana State Pirogues Racing Champion in his youth and was quite proud of it. Pirogues are as Louisiana as Cajuns are, and pirogues have played a role in the lives of Cajuns for centuries.

Used primarily to move up and down the thousands of bayou canals that crisscross the southern Louisiana swamps, a pirogue is a small narrow-keeled boat similar to a canoe but less stable, as canoes have a flatter bottoms. They weigh only about 70 pounds and can hold two people comfortably. Usually all that is needed to propel one is a single paddle.

I had been bugging Leon for weeks to go fishing with me, and one afternoon there remained no reason not to. We loaded the pirogue into the bed of the Econoline and went to the bait shop to grab bait and a case of cold beer.

We then drove south towards New Orleans and found a good place to put into a canal. The area was desolate and beautiful. The canal banks were lined with low overhanging trees dripping long strands of grey Spanish moss from their branches. The water was tea-colored and the current was lazy.

We slid the pirogue loaded with rods and reels and our tackle boxes into the water and Leon got in the front. I pushed us off and jumped in the rear. Leon paddled us out into the canal's current and we began to drift with it downstream.

I opened a beer with my church key and handed it to him. I opened one for myself, set it between my feet and began to fiddle with my rod. I baited a hook and cast along the bank and let the bait settle. He did the same. Little was said between us for some time except when someone needed a beer or a smoke. We were too busy watching the egrets and water birds and just taking in the scenery.

Pretty soon, Leon said, "I'm gonna teach you how to pee off a pirogue." I laughed and said, "I'm game." With that, he set his beer down and began to stand. He positioned his feet securely against each side of the tippy little boat.

The pirogue started to gently rock from side-to-side but he was able to control it by simply flexing his knees. I sat very still and watched. He stood there for a long time, watching his stream enter the water. He finished, shivered a little, zipped up his pants and sat slowly down. "There. When you gotta go, do it that way." I shook my head in agreement.

Well, I had been fine up until then and hadn't felt the urge.

But after three beers and watching him do it, I felt like I was standing at the base of Angel Falls, in the Guayana highlands of Venezuela where a zillion gallons of water comes down in a free fall of 979 meters from the Churum River. I had to pee. The problem was I wasn't a past Louisiana State Pirogue Champion. Leon was sitting in the front facing away from me. I said, "Now, I'm gonna pee." He grunted an approval.

So, I slowly stood, but I forgot the part about placing each foot securely against the sides. I was standing with both feet close together and unzipped and aimed overboard. The boat tilted in the direction I aimed. I stepped quickly back to counter the roll and the little boat rocked violently in that direction in the flash of an eye. Leon hollered, "Hey, what the..." It was too late.

Water rushed into the side that I had stepped back towards. To counter that, I quickly stepped in the other direction still trying to pee. Water rushed into the other side. Leon didn't dare stand and was yelling at me to sit down. But I couldn't because I was very busy trying to counteract each roll of the boat. Finally, after violently rocking the boat back and forth several times, enough water had entered the boat that it slowly sank underneath us. It was hopeless.

The water wasn't very deep and our tackle boxes started floating away along with empty beer cans. We both stood up and took a step into the mucky bottom as the boat rolled completely over and popped back up, upside down, and floated there next to us.

Neither one of us said anything -- we just looked at each other. Leon thought the whole thing was funny, as did I, and we started laughing while we tried to get boat upright. Every time we tried to roll it upright, it refilled with water then proceeded to sink and pop back up beside us upside down. We finally elected to drag it to the bank.

About the time we made that decision, two local folks walked across a far dirt berm, a pole on their shoulders slung between them. On the pole hung a seven foot alligator, and it all of a sudden hit us where we were and what could be in the water beneath us. Up to then, we hadn't given that any thought. That caused us to go into a wild, thrashing, boat-dragging, foot-slogging, slow-running underwater race for the bank and safety.

We were finally able to retrieve the tackle boxes and a little of the remaining beer to drink on the way home. We were sopping wet, a little drunk, hungry, but we were having our kind of fun. About midway home, I had to pee again. I asked Leon to pull the truck over to the side of the road. I got out and stood close to the side of the truck and unzipped. Just as the flow started, Leon hollered, "Hey! Don't swamp the God damn truck!" I had to laugh.

But, the boredom was broken for another day.

Periodically, when times were lean, we did other flying jobs to fill in the blanks.

At certain times of the year, the Louisiana Department of Agriculture and Forestry would leave a specially equipped Cessna 172 with us and contracted us to fly it for them. The job was fire-spotting.

Some days we did routine patrol watching for and reporting forest fires; other days, we were called in to overfly a fire in progress and find routes into it that the firefighters and heavy equipment could use to access it. We loved doing it mostly because we could legally flat-hat low across the tree tops when we wanted to and nobody had anything to say about it.

There was one problem about doing it that, fortunately, Leon and I both had a common immunity against, and that was the turbulence. Fires create fierce amounts of turbulence generated by the rising columns of heat over them. In order to spot the men and equipment into the fire, you had to fly down into that turbulence.

If you weren't seat-belted in very tightly, it was a sure bet you'd wind up getting slammed all over the cabin. It was so violent at times that just keeping aircraft straight and level was a workout. So, it really took two people to do the job – one to fly, the other to man the radios. Neither one of us was ever prone to air or sea sickness, even in roughest air or water.

Air and sea sickness is highly contagious.

When I was transferred to Germany from FT. Bragg, North Carolina, in 1963, they sent everybody with orders to Europe on transport ships. Those ships were the old Liberty class troop transport ships produced during World War II. These ships usually had as many as 3,800 men crammed onto them.

I never had a problem. I was always hungry and enjoyed the pitching and rolling of the North Atlantic seas in the wintertime. The other 3,799 guys? Not so much. Most of them were violently seasick by the time we exited New York harbor and stayed that way until we docked in Germany nine days later. I took great glee in starting chain reaction vomits.

I would spot some poor soul on the verge of throwing up and trying his best to stifle it. I would then bolt to the rail and make retching noises as loudly as I could. In turn, said victim would hit the rail, followed by at least two or three others in close proximity that had succumbed to his vomiting. I would walk away chuckling to myself.

I played this game for nine days. The great part was that very few men were ever hungry, and I could eat all I wanted.

Eating was great fun, too. You went through a chow line, got your food on a metal tray and took a seat at a long shiny Formica topped table with a little guard rail built around the table's edge. Its purpose was to stop things from sliding off during heavy, pitching seas. One of my favorite activities was to watch half sea sick men trying eat off of sliding trays. After several attempts at trying to keep a moving mess tray from sliding away, most of them just gave up, dumped their tray into the trash and went to the head. On day one, I had perfected the ability to hold the tray with one hand and eat with the other. I never had a problem and loved Navy chow. Well, actually, I loved any chow then.

By the time we arrived in Germany, the USNS Patch should been renamed the USNS Barf because it was just a big floating tub of vomit.

Back at the airport. We always had several people that hung around and were sort of like groupies. They came and went. Most of them didn't jump, but for whatever reason, they loved hanging out and being in the way. One, a young kid named Tommy was actually very helpful and did things like sweeping and cleaning up for free. He eventually did become a jumper. But others that that we attracted were mostly annoying.

There were two young girls, teenagers, who started hanging around in the late summer. They constantly bugged us to take them flying. One day, they had badgered Leon to the point of tears. Just then, we got a call to go check out a fire. I saw the light bulb come on over his head. He looked at me and grinned. I emphatically shook my head, *No. No. NO!*

He would not be dissuaded. He hung up the phone and looked at the girls and said, "Okay. We'll take you up, but just this once. And, I have one demand."

The girls looked at each other giggling. One of the girls said, "What?"

Leon then said, "Listen. It might very rough over that fire and you might get airsick."

The girls looked at each other quizzically. "If you throw up, you have to clean it up."

They both simultaneously, enthusiastically said, "Okay!"

I was still shaking my head in disbelief. Leon rummaged around in the desk drawer and came up with two sick bags and demonstrated their use. We headed for the airplane. We put the girls in the back seat and very tightly belted them in. They were all smiley and silly.

As I crawled in the co-pilot's seat up front, I glanced back at them and they looked like two children who had just entered Wonderland. Their eyes were all big and wide. As Leon got in and buckled up he gave them some further instructions about not talking, not moving around and making sure their seat belts were super tight.

We took off and headed for the fire. Once over it, we did the usual things maneuvering around it, calling equipment in, looking for egress routes, etcetera. We paid little attention to the girls save an occasional glance and smile to ensure they were okay.

They were doing surprisingly well and I started to breathe a sigh of relief. It was bumpy, but not violently so -- except for the occasional hard hit -- but we had experienced infinitely worse in the past. Fuel started to run low, and we peeled off and headed back to refuel and drop the girls off.

We landed with the wheels giving their little noise of protest as the landing gear touched down. They girls were both quiet, and I told them they could unbuckle if they wanted, which they both did.

They hadn't said word one since we took off. Just as we taxied up to the gas pump, out of the corner of my eye, I saw one of the girls raise a bag to her face. In a split second, she let go into the bag. The other one's reaction was instantaneous and explosive.

Little chunks of stuff flew past me and splattered all over the instrument panel, some of it hit the backs of our heads, and rest of it covered the backs of our seats with a vile oozing mess. I bailed out my side, Leon did the same.

We just stood there looking at them in amazement except that I was the one with the *I TOLD you so!!* look on my face. The girls were both sobbing and we felt sorry for them. Leon told them to go over to the little public bathroom and wash up. We'd get started cleaning up the airplane.

They washed up and came back to the plane and kept their promise and helped us clean up and deodorize the cabin. Once we finished, Leon and I bade them good-bye, refueled the bird and took off again.

As we taxied for take-off, it was quiet between us. I was flying this time and he had the radios. We lifted off and headed in the direction of the fire. En route we didn't talk -- none of the usual banter.

He knew I wanted to say it just to piss him off. But I didn't. With the fire in sight, he reached over to pick up a mike. I just busted out laughing about that time. He started laughing, too. As he brought the mike up to say something, he said, half snickering, "Just don't say it."

"Say what?" I said.

"That I'm a dumb-ass."

"I don't have to. You just did."

He nodded and we went to work doing what we did best – and that was to operate as a team.

Chapter Twelve

Why We Jump?

Why would anybody strap a parachute on their back and jump out of a perfectly good airplane?

I've heard that refrain probably a thousand times over the years, and my response was always the same: Why shouldn't you?

Let me give you a few good reasons.

Have you ever stood on a summer's day and looked up at the towering white cumulus clouds in the sky? If they are cumulonimbus, they are building thunderstorm clouds of stark white that may billow up 50,000 feet or so. In short order, rain will begin to fall somewhere.

Well, imagine circling those clouds as they build, looking out over them from your perch in the airplane, but unlike those on the ground, you are looking into them, not up at them.

If you are a pilot, you can fly alongside them, touching them with your wing tips, as if they are some great, misty-white beluga whale and you are a tiny swimmer treading alongside.

If you are a jumper, your pilot can continue to skirt them climbing ever higher until, at last, you jump, prone yourself into an arch and plummet alongside the cloud as if falling into a great, deep canyon at speeds greater than 120 miles-an-hour. You will have the smell of fresh rain in your nostrils as you do.

Falling alongside the bulging cloud walls will exhilarate your senses. You will feel separated from anything that pecks or nags at you below, and none of that will matter for the moment.

I made my first sky-dive, not military drop, there's a difference, at Ft. Bragg, North Carolina. Ft. Bragg had three separate sport parachute clubs: one that catered to the troops of the XVIII Airborne Corps, which was me at the time, one that was specifically for the troops of the 82nd Airborne Division (which would be me later), and, finally, one for the various Special Forces Groups at Ft. Bragg. They all did exactly the same thing.

They all trained first time sport parachutists. They were all an outlet for the sky diving activities of more experienced jumpers. They all had juke boxes. They all sold beer. Why Ft. Bragg needed three clubs, I'll never know.

My club had its own aircraft, a Cessna 195 -- a high wing, single engine airplane that could carry four jumpers comfortably. It was painted Day-Glo orange. Another question, because if it ever went down on Sicily Drop Zone which is a half mile wide and two and a half miles long and doesn't have a blade of grass on its sandy surface, you could have found it by feel. If you jumped and missed Sicily, you should have been flogged.

Many of the senior club members would later become parachuting super stars. Some of them would jump with the U.S. Army Parachute Team, the world famous Golden Knights. Others would become major parachuting innovators. Still others would become world champions.

A buddy of mine had urged me to come with him and take the first jump course at XVIII Airborne Corps Sport Parachute Club, which I did, in 1962.

We were already young Airborne troopers and thought it would be a walk in the park. Aha! But there's a difference between being basically pushed out the door at 1,200 feet on a military drop from a C130 and free fall on a sport jump from much higher altitudes.

As a sport parachutist, the difference was greater still as we got more experience, and the altitude would get as high as 12,500 feet and higher still later on.

There are some other differences. First, there is speed. A military airborne drop takes place very quickly. You stand up, hook up your static line, shuffle to the door, you go out the door and you build up no appreciable speed. Your parachute is automatically opened by the static line, and presto, you are under a large olive drab canopy.

A sport parachutist, a skydiver, after training, goes out the door into free fall. Within 12 seconds or so, a skydiver will have reached a descent speed of 120 miles-an-hour while using a stable arch body position. In other body positions, much higher speeds can be reached. The speed is more evident in your ears and the whipping of your jumpsuit. The fun part is the speed and varying body positions that allow you to move around and across the sky.

The next difference is the ground rush. You don't usually experience the scariness of the ground coming up at you, fast, on a military jump. That is, unless you were under a "streamer," a malfunctioned parachute.

In that case, you are busy fighting for your life, and how fast the ground is coming at you is secondary. Just getting under your reserve parachute will be all that matters. Period.

Ground rush is a sensation that takes place in free fall. You may be at 10,000 feet experiencing the excitement of falling with your arms and legs outstretched, the wind roaring in your ears, and looking out on the far horizon which can appear to be the very edge of space -- but it really isn't.

When you look at the ground below, the patchwork of it will appear basically the same at any very high altitude. But, at a certain point, usually below 2,500 feet, if you haven't opened your parachute yet, the ground will suddenly leap into your face, Phoom!, with frightening close-up detail.

It happens for different folks at different altitudes, at or below 2,500 feet. I was cocky and many times jumped with no altimeter, nothing to measure altitude. My ground rush always happened to me in the vicinity of 1,700 feet. So, I knew where I was. It was plenty of time to open and handle any problems that might exist such as a malfunctioning canopy.

Next, being under an open canopy is different. Military parachute jumps normally take place in very crowded skies. There can be hundreds of men in the air at one time and they all have very limited means of staying away from each other. Troop canopies have nowhere near the kind of control and steering ability a sport canopy does.

Entanglements and possible death from collapsed canopies are common -- less so today, than in times past. It's a busy time for a military jumper, keeping his head on a swivel and anticipating a landing with maybe 70 to 100 extra pounds of gear and weapons attached to him. Landings can be very hard and injuries are common.

But for a sport parachutist, being under a parachute is much different. There are fewer people with you in the air, maybe only a couple. That changes when mass exits involving 50 to 100 skydivers take place. But normally, there is time to look around and enjoy the ride and the beauty of the landscape beneath. And, today, landings are not much harder than jumping off of a kitchen table.

But, for me, the best answer I can give to the question, "Why do you jump?" follows.

In the beginning, it was all about adventure, the thrill, and the temporary feeling of being completely alive. You become addicted to those few moments of free fall and the parachute ride where every nook and corner of you is, at once, free, completely alive and whole. Then, after a time, while that does not go away, a new sensation starts to take place -- the feeling of belonging.

My father was an only child, a loner. He brought that into his marriage and parenthood. Consequently, we were never close. He had his hobbies to keep him occupied, and it was pretty much every-man-for-himself growing up. Oh, he made the occasional feeble attempt at shooting the .22 rifle together or maybe going fishing with me, but it was always short-lived.

I don't hold it against him now. He's gone. In retrospect, I know that he had no real family background and simply didn't know what's important to children. But, it did have a net effect on me and that was due to not having anybody there to fawn over my successes and help me with my failures. Life was all on me and I wasn't very good at it. I failed a lot early on.

But, I became very good at flinging myself out of airplanes. I became accepted into the clique that was sport parachuting. I made many friends there, some of whom, I am still in touch with today some 30 years later. It became my fraternity. They put up with and accepted my eccentricities, and we lived life together through the great times and the bad times. Leon was "family" and a man I considered a brother for many years. Still do.

As the years passed, I got to know hundreds and hundreds of jumpers and visited many drop zones across the country. The jumpers there knew of me and I knew of them. There were, unfailingly, offers of drink, food and lodging. We were all a special family separated from the cares of the earth-bound. It would shape me and complete me and give me my sense of values and mold me into someone I would not be afraid to die with.

So, if you ask me today, why did you jump? It was for all those reasons. I think that if you ask any of the jumpers who have stayed in the sport for any length of time, or who are still at it today, their answers will be basically the same.

They will at some point reveal to you that sky divers, sport parachutists, or whatever name you want to give them, are all part of a very special extended family. Family members come and go, die off, have families, and sometimes do something stupid and get hurt for it, but down the road, there is always that bond.

A special bond.

Epilogue

The Last Exit at Hammond
Into the Best Job I Ever Had

In 1969, I had been at Hammond for nearly four years. I was 24 years old – and restless. During my time there, I had trained well over 1000 first jump students, made in excess of 1,200 jumps and had racked up thousands of hours of pilot-in-command time in various aircraft. I had begun a working career as a jumper that would span 20 years.

But at Hammond, in 1969, I began to look at reentering the military. Viet Nam was raging and the soldier in me had developed dreams of becoming a door gunner on a Huey helicopter. I snuck off one day and visited a recruiter.

During my first stint in the U.S. Army, I had encountered a few problems and the recruiter informed me that a waiver from the Pentagon was needed for me to re-enlist. So we filed the various pieces of paperwork and obtained the personal letters of recommendation that were required and I waited.

Over the course of the years, many military jumpers had visited Hammond to jump. Among them was a full-bird U.S. Army Colonel named Waldie. I never knew his first name. He was an Irish Catholic Chaplain.

When he visited, he always had with him several junior officers from the Fort Polk, Louisiana, Sport Parachute Club. We got along famously. I never figured my reenlistment would have a role for these guys.

After a few months of waiting, the recruiter walked in the door one day and said, "You ready?" I stood there blankly staring at him before the question sunk in. When it did, I bounded across the room and shook his hand. I would leave for New Orleans and in-processing in a few days. I had already said my good-byes to Leon and Prissy. They were supportive of my reenlistment.

The day came to leave, and a girlfriend drove me to the bus station for the trip to New Orleans recruiting station for in-processing and swearing in. Then, the plan was to go from New Orleans to Fort Polk for basic training again. I had been out too long since my first hitch, and had to retake basic training. I looked forward to it.

Once I graduated at Fort Polk, I would be sent to Fort Rucker, Alabama, to Crew Chief's School there for eight weeks and then, hopefully, to the Far East. Crew Chiefs served as door gunners on "Hueys" -- the Bell HU-1B Iroquois helicopter. I was ready to get me a machine gun and rain death down on the Viet Cong from above.

I got New Orleans out of the way and they bused a group of us to Fort Polk and the induction station. Once at the induction center, you could expect three days of haircuts, shots, physical examinations, uniform issue and harassment from guys who were bigger pricks than I would become in a few days. I'll explain that shortly.

The second day at the induction center, I remembered that Colonel Waldie and his guys were somewhere on Fort Polk. I started asking around as to the whereabouts of the officer's quarters. As it turned out, there were a number of officers' bungalows adjacent to the induction center.

The first few free minutes I got, I walked over there and started looking at the name plates on the screen doors. Sure enough, there was Colonel Waldie's name on one of the first doors I came to. I could hear someone singing inside. I knocked and waited.

In a minute, Colonel Waldie shuffled to the door in flip-flops with a towel wrapped around his waist. He had been in the shower.

He saw that it was me and he smiled. I snapped to attention and flipped him a crisp salute, grinning. He said, "Well, I'll be damned. You're a soldier again." We made small talk and caught up, and then it was time for me to get back.

As I was leaving, he shouted behind me, "Hey! Mike. Do you know what training company they've assigned you to?" I stopped and said, "Yes, sir. E-4-2" "Okay. We'll look you up." "Great!" I said and continued on back to the induction center.

From there, it was all business. They moved us up to the company area in semi-trailers. The cadre, the Drill Sergeants, were all buck Sergeants, three stripers, who had seen combat in Viet Nam. They quickly found out that I was prior service and as a result, they called me into the day room the second day at E-4-2.

All of the Drill Sergeants had gathered there along with the Company Commander, a First Lieutenant. When I walked through the door, they were silent at first and I just stood there at attention.

"Mike. Relax. We've got a proposal for you." said one of the Drill Sergeants. I took a parade rest stance with my hands behind my back and my feet spread to shoulder width like the book says. "Naw. Relax more. This ain't an inquisition." said another one of the Drill Sergeants. The Company Commander was just sitting there listening.

"Look. We pulled your records. They show that you were Airborne and also Military Police." I shook my head in the affirmative. "Well, here's the deal. We know you don't need to go back through all of this again, so here's what we are going do."

I listened. "Those guys out there are a mix of draftees and volunteers. The draftees are usually older and more mature, ready to just get their two years over with and go back home. They'll pretty much keep their mouths shut and go along with the program. It's the R.A.'s, Regular Army types, the volunteers, who are younger, more gung-ho, but have never really been leaned on before. They're the ones we'll have to stay after. They're the ones who will screw up first and the most."

I nodded in agreement. He went on, "You're different. You're prior military, experienced, and you've been around a bit." I nodded again.

"Here's what we're going to do if you're up to it." He reached out and handed me a set of Sergeant's stripes. If you agree, we're going make you the Field First Sergeant for the time you are here. Consider yourself a Drill Sergeant." I was stunned and all happy-faced.

I said, "Roger."

He went on, "Now for appearance's sake, we have to make it at least "look" like you are going through training, but your real job is going to be maintaining discipline. You do it in whatever fashion you choose -- if it takes falling the whole bunch of 'em out at 0300 to do push-ups, so be it. If you need to throw bunks out of windows, do it...get the picture?" I said, "Yes." I had just been appointed Master Prick. I lived up to it.

We all went out where the entire company was standing in formation. All the Drill Sergeants and I went up on a riser to address them. The lead Drill Sergeant spoke first. "You boys know who we are -- we introduced ourselves to you yesterday."

Then he looked at me and continued, "Now, I want to introduce you to our newest Drill Sergeant, Marcon here. He's ex-Airborne Military Police. He's now a Drill Sergeant and your Field First Sergeant.

You will answer to him, the same as you would to any of us. He's first in your chain-of-command before us." He paused. "Got any questions?"

Silence.

Then he looked at me again and asked me if I had anything to say. I stepped forward and said, "Yes. I do."

I looked out across the company and said, "For the next eight weeks, if you do it right, you won't know me. Do it wrong, fuck it up, you're gonna get to know me real well and you ain't gonna like it."

With that I stepped back, and basic training for the men of E-4-2 began in earnest. I took my new job seriously. I thought then that I had just been handed the best job I would ever have. But I was wrong. The best was still ahead.

Things rolled along pretty well. The Drill Sergeants were right. The draftees buckled down and did a good job. The R.A.s were the ones I had to go after the most. But, gradually, most of them began to come around. Oh, bunks did fly out windows, and there were 0300 push-up sessions.

But as the weeks rolled by -- weeks filled with classroom work, 10 and 30 mile forced marches through the piney woods and down dusty roads, time spent firing on the ranges, sessions in tear gas filled rooms learning how to use gas masks, inspections, learning how to disassemble and reassemble a rifle blindfolded – the men really started to shape up.

By the end of the fifth week, morale got even higher as graduation loomed on the horizon, usually followed by some leave time home. I was on-fire gung-ho. At the start of the sixth week, we were in the field one morning learning to fight with pugil sticks -- think broom handles with boxing gloves on each end. The exercise is meant to mimic bayonet fighting.

Just then, a jeep screamed up behind us, stopped, and a Corporal got out hollering my name. "Yo!" I said and raised my hand. He ran up to me and said there was a full-bird Colonel waiting for me back in orderly room. The first thought I had was, *Oh! Shit, I've pissed off some Congressman's kid.* I had forgotten all about Waldie.

"Com'on, we gotta go fast." the Corporal barked. I jumped in the jeep and he drove like a bat out of hell back to post. I had no idea what was up and the Corporal didn't know either.

When I came through the door, the poor Company Commander was standing up against the back wall looking like somebody was about to shoot his dog. The Colonel was standing with his back to me then he turned to face me. It was Waldie. I breathed a sigh of relief then reached out to shake his hand.

"Relax, Lieutenant, the soldier and I are friends." said Waldie. The C.O. disappeared into his office.

Waldie and I walked outside. Then he said, "How would you like to come to Houston with a few of us and make some jumps at Doc's Anognostis's place?" I said that I would. He then said, "I'll make arrangements with the Lieutenant in there and we'll pick you up bright and early Saturday morning. We'll bring gear for you."

I thanked him and he got in his car and left. Just then, the company came marching back into the company area for lunch. I turned and went to the mess hall.

I was waiting at the orderly room door Saturday morning when a bright orange Dodge Super-Bee pulled up and three people got out. They were Colonel Waldie, First Lieutenant Polaski and Captain Balzegar. They had brought civilian clothes for me which I quickly changed in to.

We headed for Houston. As we drove, questions started coming my way.

Did I have my commercial pilot's license?

Yes.

Was I a parachute rigger?

Yes.

Was I interested in becoming the manager and pilot of the Fort Polk Sport Parachute Club?

"WHAT? YES!"

Unbeknown to me at the time, Waldie had some strings pulled and already had my orders to Fort Rucker cancelled and had me reassigned to Fort Polk in his unit. After I said "yes," they told me so. This was too good to pass up, no matter how badly I wanted to kill Viet Cong.

Another two weeks passed and the company graduated from basic training. The vast majority of the guys would get leave. After leave, many of them would return to North Fort Polk, "Tiger Land," the Advanced Infantry Training Center -- for another eight weeks of training. From there, most of them would go directly to Viet Nam as replacements and whatever fate awaited them.

I would go to Tiger Land as well for that was where the club was located. But, my fate would be entirely different from any of theirs.

Entirely different.

So, here is the set-up. I answered to no one except for Waldie. I would wear civilian clothes excluding when a uniform was absolutely necessary for a special event. I would live in the club building in a private room set up just for me.

I would eventually be sent back to Houston to take delivery of a brand new burgundy and white Cessna 180, which I have always thought of as the best all-around airplane ever produced. I fell in love with it.

The reason for that was that Colonel Waldie, the club's senior officer and the Ft. Polk airfield commander were always at each other's throats. They were in disagreement over the business of the club using military aircraft and military pilots on the week-ends like every other club in the U.S. Army did. So every week-end, the airfield commander would "red-line" (ground) every aircraft and helicopter he had just to keep the club from having their use.

So, after I took over the club, we just went out and leased our own. I could fly that 180 to anywhere at any time I wanted at no charge -- except when we needed it on the week-ends.

Furthermore, the set-up included managing the club bar and its always full walk-in beer cooler, having full control of who came and went, training first jump students, and getting to jump with and know the craziest bunch of jumpers that ever lived.

Viet Nam was still out there, but, for the foreseeable future, I was going to get to do the best job anyone ever had. And, I enjoyed it to a fault, every last second of it. I had just been handed the cushiest skydiving job in the United States Army. My time there is the subject of another book.

11504233R0009

Made in the USA
Lexington, KY
09 October 2011